EXCELLENCE IN TEACHING

EXCELLENCE IN TEACHING

NARRATIVES FROM AWARD-WINNING FACULTY

EDITED BY

MARIANNE CASTANO BISHOP

GWENDOLYN METTETAL

P. N. SAKSENA

Wolfson Press
Indiana University South Bend

Special Thanks

John Garrido, student in Integrated Media Studies, for designing our book cover.

Barbara Mociulski, Senior Lecturer in Fine Arts, for helping us hold a student competition in her class for our book cover and mentoring our winner John Garrido.

Marcia Holland, Associate Faculty of English, for her expert skills in preliminary editing and proofreading.

Kael Kanczuzewski, Instructional Technology Specialist at UCET (now Principal Digital Learning Consultant at IUPUI), for page design and layout.

David James and Ken Smith of IU South Bend's Wolfson Press, for their patient InDesign work.

Thank you to the following individuals for their assistance with the campus one-time funds used for the publication of this book:

Former IU South Bend Chancellor Una Mae Reck
Anurag Pant and Jerry Hinnefeld: Co-chairs of the Academic Senate Budget Committee.

ISBN 978-1979310130

Wolfson Press
Master of Liberal Studies Program
Indiana University South Bend
1700 Mishawaka Avenue
P.O. Box 7111
South Bend IN 46634-7111
wolfson.iusb.edu

Contents

Preface

I congratulate our faculty whose essays are featured in this book. They are dedicated and committed to their craft and to the success of their students. In recognition of their teaching excellence, they have received one or more prestigious teaching awards at our campus or at the all-IU level. Through these essays, they share experiences and emotions that will touch and inspire you.

I thank the editors of this book for their vision and for sharing narratives from our faculty with others. These essays let people know how thoughtful and reflective our faculty are and how they continue to build a successful community of practitioners.

Dr. Jann L. Joseph
Executive Vice Chancellor for Academic Affairs
Indiana University South Bend

Introduction

Marianne Castano Bishop

Since this is a book of narratives, I start with a story of how this book evolved. Several years ago, I served as the Instructional Strategist at the University Center for Excellence in Teaching (UCET) at Indiana University South Bend. I had frequent one-on-one consultations with faculty and conducted seminars and workshops for faculty development. Through the years, many of our faculty shared their personal and professional stories with me — stories that were packed with excellent instructional strategies as well as their struggles and challenges. In fact, the strategies had often arisen as a result of their struggles. When I became the Distance Learning Program Manager and was promoted to Founding Director of the Center for Distance Education (now Center for Online Education), I continued to have profound conversations with our faculty, who shared their narratives with me.

The art and science of teaching and learning has always fascinated me. I enjoy working with faculty and also teaching. While serving as administrator throughout my higher education career, I found a different degree of fulfillment when I was also teaching. When I was a doctoral student, I sought every opportunity to serve as a teaching fellow.

Like the authors in this book, I have written peer-reviewed and other scholarly articles. This time, though, I wanted to embark on a project that was different and unique and would showcase our faculty. I enjoy story-telling and believe that sharing our stories, albeit in various intensities and dimensions, could be therapeutic and inspirational almost at the same time. The question that was on my mind for a while was — what if we could capture narratives in a book for more people to read, particularly from our award-winning faculty? I wanted a book of narratives where the written text flowed naturally from the authors' hearts, minds, and souls.

Many of us enjoy reading books and watching movies. We are inevitably connected by stories. We tend to organize our experiences, knowledge, and thinking through stories, so I was not surprised to find out from scholars that our brains are hardwired to think in narratives. Stories can be powerful in presenting our individual and collective truths.

A wonderful opportunity arose when the IU South Bend Academic Senate Budget Committee had a call for proposals for one-time funding. Perfect timing! Several weeks after I submitted the application, I received the good news. So armed with funding for publication I sought the assistance and support of two multi-award winning faculty members to serve as co-editors with me — P.N. Saksena and Gwynn Mettetal. We started inviting IU South Bend faculty who had won major campus or all-IU teaching awards to share their personal narratives as well as instructional practices.

My co-editors and I are proud that we have embarked on several firsts through this book: 1) first book of narratives from our award-winning faculty, 2) first book of its kind to be published by our campus publisher Wolfson Press, and 3) first such project to receive campus funding support.

We hope you will find your own special meaning that touches you in some profound way from the narratives. The authors added their own ingredients and spiced them up — some with humor, others with emotion, and many with information. You will, I hope, find that nugget of wisdom as well.

Chapter 1 - Confessions of a Former Chief Academic Officer

In "Confessions of a Former Chief Academic Officer," Alfred J. Guillaume, Jr., (Professor Emeritus of French and former Executive Vice Chancellor for Academic Affairs) features a story he often shares with our faculty, Dr. Prieto's way to motivate students. "He wrote the letter 'A' on the blackboard, declaring that every student in the class would receive an 'A' and then he would leave the 'A' on the blackboard all semester." Dr. Guillaume goes on to describe the impact of Dr. Prieto's A and what he learned along the way about teaching, working with faculty, and building alliances between faculty and administration.

Chapter 2 - Touring in High Heels: Lessons in Study Abroad

In "Touring in High Heels," Neovi Karakatsanis (Professor of Political Science) shares some of her hilarious experiences and challenges when she took her students overseas as part of a study abroad course on the European Union. Prior to the trip, she was convinced that students "would not only learn about the European Union, they would experience it." When the adventure began and students were to serve as "ambassadors of our country and our university," she designed "three practical rules of the road." She recaps the mishaps, problems, the unexpected, and the transformations.

Chapter 3 - The F-Word: The Challenges and Rewards of Facilitating Difficult Conversations

Even after more than a decade of teaching and numerous teaching awards, Elizabeth Bennion (Professor of Political Science) still goes through what many seasoned faculty members go through. In "The F-Word: The Challenges and Rewards of Facilitating Difficult Conversations," she confesses that "Every semester I worry that I will fall short in the classroom — that students will not respond well to my teaching, be inspired to push themselves out of their comfort zones, deeply engage in the course material, interact positively with their classmates, or recognize what they have learned." In allowing herself and her students to engage in a historical and contemporary debate about feminism — the "F-word" — she learned valuable lessons about moderating difficult discussions.

Chapter 4a - Teaching in Circles; Chapter 4b - Homage to a Colleague, Mentor, and Friend

Vince Peterson (Professor Emeritus of Counseling and Human Services) drafted a narrative but was not able to finish it since he passed away in that same year. Jannette (Joy) Alexander (Associate Professor Emeritus of Counseling and Human Services) wrote "An Homage to a Colleague, Mentor, and Friend," highlighting her mentor's impact on her teaching, her academic and personal life, and her counseling of students. Early in her academic career, she was hoping Dr. Peterson would tell her what to do. True to form, he did not. Pleadings to him to get a response to "How did I do?" would be met with "How do you think you did?" Her narrative pays tribute to how her mentor steered her journey from a newly-hired faculty member full of self-doubts to one who has attained her own definition of success and self-reliance.

Chapter 5 - The Passing of the Trash Can

Three weeks into the semester when she was teaching a graduate education course in classroom management for the first time, Gwendolyn (Gwynn) Mettetal (Professor of Psychology and Education) was almost in tears. In "The Passing of the Trash Can" she shares how she changed her syllabus after having a serious conversation with her students. She elaborates on the ten lessons she learned from that class.

Chapter 6 - Before Dissecting, Kiss Frog

In "Before Dissecting, Kiss Frog," Tom Vander Ven (Emeritus Professor of English) shares his observations about teaching. Early in his teaching career he learned the importance of the statement, "I don't know." He describes an inspirational teacher as "riveting, ardent, coherent, sonorous, ironic, and professorially larger than life." On the other hand, he wondered why another instructor seemed to be talking to the wall while two students listened. He observes that "[l]ooming over our classroom toil is the great frog of uncertainty."

Chapter 7 - Less Is More

Monica Tetzlaff (Associate Professor of History) learned from a master teacher mentor that good teachers "steal" from other teachers. In "Less Is More" she recounts being asked by a retiring colleague to direct his Freedom Summer Program, a two-week, three-credit Civil Rights Study Tour of several states. She made use of the resources he gave her — notes, forms, contacts, itineraries, etc. As she continued to teach the course, she decided to add more activities and resources and realized she needed to make the course her own.

Chapter 8 - Ready for Class Today?

More than two decades ago, Anne Brown (Professor of Mathematical Sciences) took on the task of redesigning and teaching the T-courses — math courses meant to "teach future elementary teachers how to explain the concepts and procedures of elementary school mathematics." In "Ready for Class Today?" she describes feeling that she was no longer reaching students effectively. She decided to step away from teaching the course, although she continued to be the T-courses coordinator. In the summer of 2011, she decided to teach a T-course face-to-face while she was developing an online version of the same course. She happily noted that online teaching in many ways revived her passion to teach T-courses.

Chapter 9 - A Teacher's To-Do Lists

In "A Teacher's To-Do Lists," Rebecca Brittenham (Professor of English) came up with several lists as she taught her graduate students in a training workshop for teachers. Her examples included "Things You Can Do with a Podium Mounted on a Table at the Front of a Classroom," "Hand/Brain Operations Involved in Teaching," and a few others. Notwithstanding having these lists, she confessed how "still inwardly anxious" she was in teaching the class. She shares what she learned about teaching, rethinking, and reconstruction.

Chapter 10 - Teaching Art My Way

After graduating with an MFA in the 1960s, Harold (Tuck) Langland (Professor Emeritus of Sculpture) found that jobs in studio art were rare, so he decided to apply abroad and landed in England as a sculpture teacher. He realized early on that, although he had the degree, he had no training in how to teach art. While in England, he adapted a teaching philosophy which he has been using throughout his teaching career. In "Teaching Art My Way," he shares what he believes is truly essential in teaching.

Chapter 11 - The More I Teach, the Less I Know

James (Jay) VanderVeen (Associate Professor of Anthropology and Sociology) started his academic career thinking that he was a good teacher since "he knew it all." In "The More I Teach, the Less I Know," he describes how very wrong he was when "sixty percent [of his students]… flat out failed" an exam. He decided to have a conversation with his students about "how their failure was [his] failure," and he made major changes in his teaching practice thereafter. Starting from a clean slate, he used web-enhanced tools, games, and other instructional strategies.

Chapter 12 - Changing My Mindset
Carolyn Schult (Associate Professor of Psychology) started her academic career as a teaching assistant who lacked confidence. She was inspired by a friend and first-time teacher, Gina, whom she described as a "great teacher." She was convinced that Gina had a "gift for teaching" and she did not. When faced with obstacles, she would default to "what would Gina do?" (WWGD). In "Changing My Mindset," she discusses how she evolved from having a fixed mindset to a growth mindset.

Chapter 13 - Utilizing Student Feedback to Improve Teaching
While Yi Cheng (Professor of Mathematical Sciences) has been teaching at IU South Bend for more than two decades, she "is still eager" to read each and every student teaching evaluation. In "Utilizing Student Feedback to Improve Teaching," she underscores that "students know their teachers much more than we give them credit for." For instance, students know if a teacher genuinely cares about their learning. Realizing that "good numerical summaries and comments do not always indicate good teaching," she found ways to hone her craft through the years.

Chapter 14 - Lessons from Unexpected Teachers
One day Patricia Lewis (Associate Faculty of Mathematical Sciences) lamented to a friend who is a special education teacher and coordinator for a Special Olympics swim team about her frustration with her students. Overhearing the conversation, one of the athletes remarked that "sometimes math is hard — maybe you should talk about something else." This wise counsel sparked a series of explorations on how to teach effectively. In "Lessons from Unexpected Teachers," she recounts what she learned when teaching her own daughter and teaching an undergraduate class with a student with

a disability. She found what was universally applicable to all her students, whether they had a disability or not.

Chapter 15 - Finding Myself

In "Finding Myself," Sara Sage (former Associate Professor of Education) recounts her personal journey from thinking, "I must be right since I'm an expert" to "I must be my authentic self." She describes how she "felt like a failure" several times in her academic career. Between surviving several painful life experiences and training to become a counselor later on in her academic career, she grew to view herself and her students in a more authentic way. She shares the story of her own transformation and that of her students.

Chapter 16 - Reaching Out, Building Bridges

P. N. Saksena (former Professor of Accounting) was a keen observer of effective teaching while a student and applied what he learned when he taught undergraduate and graduate courses. In "Reaching Out, Building Bridges," he describes his journey as he was learning a major teaching strategy. When he applied it in his teaching, things went well. But he was in for a shock when he failed to apply it successfully in his online teaching. He learned there was a common denominator to successfully teaching face-to-face, hybrid, and online courses.

class conversation

ideas wither
then floodgates rush
— we bathe in fresh thought

> Terry L. Allison, *Chancellor*
> *Indiana University South Bend*

CHAPTER ONE

Confessions of a Former Chief Academic Officer

Alfred J. Guillaume, Jr.

Ever since childhood, I've loved books and welcomed the worlds within that brought adventure and opened infinite possibilities. Because I was prone to reverie, and seemingly not anchored in the present, my mother often referred to me as the absent-minded professor. Upon entering the university, I had no idea what I should pursue as a major. Three of my high school years were spent in a seminary. Happily, I followed my mother's counsel to study what I enjoyed; success, she said, would follow. Because I adored reading and language, it was only natural, then, to study languages. Graduate school followed, and voilà, I found myself in a college classroom. The most memorable moments of my academic career are those before a group of students as they drilled through verb tenses or struggled with an *explication de texte*.

Many of my colleagues at the university and I have fond memories of gifted teachers from whom we've learned and whom we happily imitate. Recently retired as the executive vice chancellor for academic affairs after fourteen years, I have been asked to make a few observations about teaching excellence at Indiana University South Bend. Before I do, I'd like to make a slight digression about how I came to recognize excellence in teaching, and ultimately, how

I became a confident learner. In my formative schooling, I struggled with math and had accepted that it was a subject that I could not master. That is, until I met Dr. Prieto, a Cuban immigrant, who taught me otherwise. He believed that every student could learn and master mathematics. Initially, I scoffed at that. Non-believer that I was, I had already convinced myself that I would be content not to fail. But he said something that resonated within me. On that very first day of class, he wrote the letter "A" on the blackboard, declaring that every student in the class would receive an "A" and that he would leave the "A" on the blackboard all semester as a reminder. But he cautioned that if we did not study, we would lose the "A." Wow! No professor had ever expressed such faith in students' capacity to learn. Because he believed that I could learn mathematics, I was determined to succeed and vowed to study hard. And I did. But more important, my mind was no longer closed to learning math. Imagine my mother's surprise when at mid-semester, I had an "A" average!

Every fall semester I repeated this story at the UCET (University Center for Excellence in Teaching) faculty orientation in my greetings to the newly hired professors. Many of these professors were newly minted Ph.D. degrees; others were seasoned teachers. But it did not matter. What I wanted them to appreciate is that Indiana University South Bend is a special place where each of our students can learn and excel. As a public university, we are committed to work diligently with students at all levels of academic preparation and to help them succeed academically. And what is expected of each of the professors is that they believe, as Dr. Prieto believed, that each student *can* learn and excel.

Indiana University South Bend is blessed with gifted and talented teachers. They, like my undergraduate professor, believe passionately in student learning. And no one knows better than I. In fourteen years of reading PTR documents and personally observing classroom teaching, I can attest irrefutably to the teaching excellence of our faculty. Those teaching philosophy statements endeared the faculty to me. I connected with them as they described their teaching methods and how their teaching changed over time to accommodate the differences in student learning. With heartfelt sincerity, yet blunt honesty, they expressed doubts about techniques used and failed. They candidly admitted their frustrations in the face of student apathy and explained how eventually they succeeded in motivating students. And when students reached that "aha" moment, they shared in the students' joy. For me, as I weighed my decision to recommend favorably, or not, for tenure and/or promotion, those teaching philosophy statements were revelatory and told me more about that professor's long-term value to the university than any other documentary evidence.

As Indiana University South Bend's executive vice chancellor for academic affairs, with stewardship of complex and multi-faceted components of the academy, I considered myself primarily a teacher. I cherished and nurtured my relationship with faculty. I understood that I had much to learn from them about teaching's centrality to the academic mission of the university. What I learned from the faculty ultimately influenced how I thought about leading the university's charge of academic excellence and how I chose to lead. In retirement, I have ample time to revisit my academic leadership, the successes as well as the failures. But what remains constant for me is the special bond I felt with the faculty. To lead effectively, I had to be not from the faculty but of the faculty. That is unquestionably the most valuable lesson I learned.

If I can openly confess that I learned from the faculty, I trust that they in turn learned from me. One of the primary roles of chief academic officer is to instruct. That instruction occurred in the way I interacted with faculty and through the comportment of my office. In my annual addresses to the faculty senate, I exhorted the faculty to push beyond the limits of academic excellence, to imagine worlds yet undiscovered in both their teaching and research. I advised them never to be complacent but rather to stretch beyond the boundaries of what is possible, to think boldly and courageously about the university's future. In the making of a great university, I asked the faculty to take risks in building upon the university's strengths. As I stood before them, I urged them to shape their destiny, for I believed firmly in their extraordinary talents. I felt privileged to be one of them, for I knew it would take strong alliances between faculty and administration to meet the challenges ahead. I've often felt that the beauty of leadership is not in the doing alone, but in the doing together. And what I believed came in part from my experiences with them and from my critical analysis of their work as teachers and scholars. What I came to appreciate was that their teaching extended beyond the classroom. Students learned perhaps as much from them outside of the classroom as they did in attending lectures. And that's what I found to be a defining quality of undergraduate education here. Faculty eagerly attended to the holistic undergraduate experience through formal and informal advising. Year after year, student testimonials about their undergraduate experience recall the quality of the faculty and their close association with them.

This impact of teachers in student learning is vividly examined in this collection of essays by some of Indiana University South Bend's most effective teachers. This modest volume is a potpourri of candid reflections about the joys and frustrations of teaching. As academics, we are accustomed to learning from each other. These first-person narratives from our colleagues offer provocative insights and helpful hints to neophytes and give more senior professors an opportunity to learn from their colleagues' successes and, perhaps, adapt new strategies and techniques in their own teaching. As professors, we are continuous learners. In reading these essays, we may see ourselves and remember with a smile, or momentary chagrin, similar experiences. And, like those PTR statements on teaching, these vignettes, too, reminded me of how fortunate our students are to have such dedicated teachers who think seriously about their work. As each of us can attest, there are days when we are magnificent teachers and other days when we are not nearly so. As we mature in the classroom, we know that teaching is not instantly magical, even when there are transcending classroom moments. What we ultimately learn is that teaching is hard, disciplined work that needs constant refining, adapting, and perfecting.

Needless to say, the pillar of Indiana University South Bend's strengths as a public university is its faculty. Their dedication to teaching is legendary. Their attention to student learning is well-documented. It was a joy to have served as their vice chancellor. I am deeply grateful for all that I have learned from our magnificent faculty, and I know that our students share the same sentiment.

CHAPTER TWO

Touring in High Heels: Lessons in Study Abroad

Neovi M. Karakatsanis

The story you are about to read is true. Some of the details have been changed to protect the guilty!

I have faced many challenges as a teacher. However, without a doubt, the most challenging course I have ever taught was a study abroad course on the European Union. Requiring an extensive proposal with the Office of Overseas Study in Bloomington and necessitating the making and maintaining of contacts in Europe — contacts that would help me arrange all aspects of the trip (from homestays to institutional visits, from purchasing train tickets down to the final details of our itinerary) — the course took a good part of almost two years of my time as a young assistant professor to develop. I expected that the course would be phenomenal, a once-in-a-lifetime opportunity for my students, many of whom had rarely had an opportunity to travel outside of Indiana. After all, my limited experience traveling with students (primarily to regional conferences and local service learning assignments) had convinced me of the transformative power of experiential learning. In this course, students would not only learn about the European Union, they would also experience it. Armed with a good deal of idealism, I set out with the highest of expectations.

I reasoned that my course on Europe would be demanding but rewarding. Students would participate in an intensive seminar on the European Union prior to departure (meeting as a class for several hours daily over a few weeks in South Bend), and then they would continue their studies in Brussels, Strasbourg, and Luxembourg for an additional two weeks. In Europe, students would follow a schedule of daily lectures and institutional visits and meetings with officials and staff members of the European Parliament and other European institutions, and participate in daily cultural training and discussion sessions. To be more fully immersed in European culture, my students would also live with a Belgian family in Brussels. And, to enhance their study of language, an optional language component would make it possible for them to attend classes in the language they were already studying at Indiana University South Bend, thanks to the good work of the Alliance Française (French), the Goethe Institut (German), and the Instituto Cervantes (Spanish), all of which had agreed to offer courses to my students. Finally, to prepare for this life-changing experience, students would be required to do a good deal of reading on the European Union and European politics prior to departure. They would keep a journal of essays covering all aspects of the course — the readings, lectures, field trips, and round table discussions. The course would culminate with a number of cultural excursions in Belgium, a free weekend for students to travel on their own in Europe, and a final weekend prior to our homecoming visiting Paris, the City of Lights. Every last detail of the course had been painstakingly planned with absolutely nothing left to chance — or so I thought.

My course, "The Politics of the European Union," began at Indiana University South Bend with a series of lectures, presentations, and class discussions. In our pre-departure meetings, we covered everything from the substance of European politics, history, and culture, to appropriate attire, comfortable walking shoes, courteousness in group travel, and then some. Because of this careful preparation, I assumed that my students' experience would be *magnifique,* and that they would have no one but me to thank for it! Not a thing would go wrong. How could it—as I had shared with them, among a mass of academic information, three eminently practical rules of the road?

Rule Number 1: Europeans do not dress as casually as we do in America. Therefore business-casual attire is most appropriate.

> *As we will be visiting a variety of political institutions and meeting many officials and other dignitaries, proper dress is required! Students should dress comfortably—yet neatly and appropriately!* ***Professional attire is strongly recommended.***

I made it a point during our pre-departure orientation to emphasize the importance of comfortable walking shoes (more on this later) and appropriate attire, emphasizing to my students that we would be visiting official European institutions—the European Commission and Parliament, the Council of Ministers, Europe's Court of Justice, the European Court of Human Rights, and the Council of Europe. I coached my class on the importance of leaving our European hosts with a good impression of us (and our university). As one of my students later reflected, we would be serving as "ambassadors of our country and our university," and appearance was an important part of the impression we would leave behind. Among the many "noes" on my list—no shorts, no American insignia (we were in the midst of post-9-11 days, when American travelers were being advised against overt displays of patriotism), no baseball caps, no athletic shoes — there were few allowances.

For whatever reason, this "proclamation" of mine — "proper dress is required" — seemed to be the cause of much consternation and concern for my students. I failed to notice this, however, consumed as I was with preparations. Perhaps I should have been more in tune when I heard that several students were keeping close tabs on my own teaching attire, trying to figure out how "a European" might dress. Another hint might have been departure day, when one young man showed up at the airport wearing a baseball cap, an American eagle emblazoned in red, white, and blue on the front of it, and the words, "PLAY TIME," stamped across his baggy sweat pants. While my temper flared, the passive aggressive in me decided against confrontation. Instead, upon our arrival at Brussels National Airport, when my disheveled student finally asked for some time to change out of his travel attire and into something more appropriate, I dug in my heels, insisting there was no time: "We have to catch our train immediately." And with this rather inauspicious start, our adventure began.

Rule Number 2: Wear Comfortable Walking Shoes.

This study abroad course will require a good deal of walking in a variety of European cities and towns. While students will rely on public transportation (usually the metro) to get to and from their places of residence and the educational building in Brussels and elsewhere, they should be prepared for a 5-15 minute walk to the metro each way. Please wear comfortable non-athletic walking shoes. When sightseeing, students will be required to do a good deal of walking on pavement that is often uneven (such as on cobblestone). While relatively leisurely, these walks can be tiring and some students have complained of blistered feet and parched lips! Students are encouraged to wear comfortable walking shoes on such days, to carry bottled water with them, and to bring a supply of "moleskin" (bandages especially formulated for blistered feet). These bandages are readily available in U.S. and European pharmacies.

While the rule regarding business-casual attire caused only a few problems, just about every student in the class seemed to misinterpret this recommendation for footwear. On the one hand, my female students were convinced their high-heeled sandals and stiletto pumps were the only appropriate shoes for their business attire, while, on the other hand, the young men, taking my advice against athletic shoes to heart, had shopped for new, stiff leather-soled shoes that would become the source of countless sores and blisters. What a predicament! What I had painstakingly planned to be fun and relaxing cultural excursions — the architectural Art Nouveau and comic strip tours in Belgium (Brussels being the birthplace of comic-strip hero Tintin), a stroll along the canals of medieval Bruges, or a walk along the Seine on our way to the Eiffel Tour — turned out to be all but torture for virtually every single one of my students. Never before had I heard so many complain so strenuously about tired, sore, blistered, and bleeding feet. And never before had I spent so much time making emergency runs with my students to the local pharmacies of every European city we visited. Soon, my students began to ask why I had not arranged for a bus and driver to get us around Europe. Rather than focusing on the cost effectiveness and sustainability of public transportation, or the obvious fact that these were common modes of travel in Europe (we were, after all, learning about Europe and its people in the course), I could not help but quip that, had I done as they were suggesting, the bus (with all of us in it) would surely have gotten wedged in one of the narrow, cobblestone alleys of Bruges that we were visiting that day. My students failed to see the humor in this retort, but our adventure continued.

Rule Number 3: Please pack lightly: one small suitcase only.

When traveling by train between cities and countries, students must be able to carry their own luggage on and off trains as well as up or down a flight of stairs (if elevators are not working or unavailable). Please pack lightly: one small suitcase only.

It goes without saying that "small" is a relative concept. I came to this realization on the day of our departure when many of my students arrived with, not large, but gargantuan luggage; luggage that was stuffed to the gills and weighing much more than any one human could reasonably lift. In addition to these students, there were also others who arrived at the airport with reasonably sized luggage but who had forgotten my warning that they should only have *one* piece of luggage, arriving with several smaller bags equally difficult to maneuver. As we traipsed around Europe, several students inevitably fell behind the group as they pushed, lugged, and kicked their luggage along, pleading (and bargaining) for assistance from others, especially when having to quickly load and unload bags onto trains, or climbing multiple flights of steps out of the Paris metro. Invariably, we risked leaving one or two students behind as they dithered about their bags while our train connections kept to a tight schedule. Soon, tempers began to flare. Students lost their patience, resenting the extra time and effort it took to help fellow travelers as we trekked across Europe. Many were beginning to complain that I should have prevented this from happening.

What More Could Go Wrong?

While I could say much more about the various "misinterpretations" of the "Physical Requirements" sheet, I won't. Nor will I share the story of how I sent fifteen of my students via train across Europe, while I remained behind in Belgium to track down two others who had gotten lost on their way to the train station — this, after detailed arrangements had been made for taxis waiting outside of each student's home on the morning of our departure with — I might add — precise information about the train station from which we would be departing. I also won't give details of the early morning call IU administrators received from two distraught students separated from our group for all of about five minutes while on a walking tour of Luxembourg City's historic district. By this point in our trip, I had come to accept that, if something could go wrong, it invariably would.

And yet, lost students, overstuffed suitcases, sore feet, and un-professional attire — those items that seemed most prominent on my list — were not the greatest challenges I faced in Europe. The real challenges, those that caused my students the greatest conster-nation and most threatened their learning experience, were often the result of personality and personal difficulties — challenges that were impossible for me to address with rules and suggestions on my "Physical Requirements" handout.

First, culture shock, a phenomenon we had discussed in our pre-departure sessions but which, nevertheless, caught several off guard, was a principal problem — one I never dreamed could raise so much trouble for so many on such a brief trip. Specifically, Europe proved to be a real challenge for several students who found themselves unable to cope with and fully appreciate the unfamiliar environment in which they found themselves—homestays with a European family quite different from their own, reliance on unfamiliar public transportation, an inability to communicate adequately in French, cuisine quite different from that served in Indiana, even different cultural expectations of formality and politeness. Faced with such differences, several of my students had a difficult time making adjustments.

Take, for example, two of my otherwise enthusiastic students who arrived at my hotel one evening, suitcases in tow, in a panic because they were sure that they had caught a whiff of marijuana at their homestay. I explained to them that, since their home was a designated nonsmoking residence and one that was typically used by our host to house Foreign Ministry officials, the offending smoke had probably wafted in from the street below through one of the open windows. This explanation didn't alleviate the students' anxiety, however; nor did my clarification that, since possession of small amounts of marijuana is legal in Belgium, it should not be a huge shock to come across this particular offending odor from time to time. This "clarification" seemed only to make matters worse. On the advice of their conservative, middle class, Hoosier parents—who probably took my explanation as some sort of implicit endorsement of soft drug use—both students insisted on moving into the hotel with me. While I hesitatingly agreed to this virtual *fait accompli*, I did so profoundly aware that these students' cultural experience would be less than complete in the absence of a homestay.

Still other students had idealized Europe. This proved to be a problem too. Expecting, in the words of one of my students, "a

Disney World fairy tale of Europe," several students were shocked to see that Europe, too, has graffiti, homelessness, pollution, and traffic congestion. Little of what I did to alleviate their difficulties — reminding them about our readings on such topics as European economic and political crises, xenophobia in Germany, sexism in Belgium, and the rise of Le Pen's extreme right in France, and encouraging them to view such "flaws" as integral to the experience — seemed to ameliorate their experience and perceptions.

I was, of course, deeply disappointed. After all, I had put more energy, effort, and concern into this course than any other I taught on campus — this, a labor of love. Faced with these challenges and, worst of all, with what I deemed to be unappreciative students, I questioned the very essence of what I was doing to promote international awareness and understanding to my students. If students were unappreciative of my efforts and unhappy with their experience abroad, then I would not offer this or any other study abroad course ever again.

But, as has often been the case with pedagogical risks I have taken, several important lessons followed — lessons I discerned as I began to read and reflect on the students' post-trip assignments. The first lesson taught to me by my students — a lesson I have learned repeatedly since then — is that an effective teacher needs to teach all of her students — not just those who demand the most attention. By focusing predominantly on the two or three most troublesome students, I had overlooked the fact that twelve or thirteen others were gaining a wealth of knowledge and experience in Europe. Indeed, several aspects of our study abroad experience — lessons that could never have been learned in the classroom and from textbooks — particularly appealed to these students. For example, in Brussels, students were delighted by our visit to the European Parliament, where they met with Madame Marie, a young assistant to a Belgian member of the European Parliament, who spent a great deal of time with my students, explaining the workings of parliament, providing them with an insider's view of daily tasks, and revealing her own professional trajectory through university education, internship, and eventual employment. Most important from the point of view of pedagogy, my students repeatedly exclaimed that they found her supranational perspective—a *French* woman, working as an assistant to a *Belgian* parliamentary member, who referred to France as *"they"* but to the EU and its parliament as *"we"*—quite interesting. (Parenthetically, one student pointed out to the entire group that Madame Marie was wearing jeans and a t-shirt while at work in Parliament—clear-cut evidence that my rule regarding professional attire was "totally bogus!")

A second highlight of the course for my students was our visit to the European Council in Strasbourg. There, in addition to visiting the Council and receiving a lecture on that institution, we were fortunate enough to arrive on a day the Council was in a special session. As a result, students were able to attend the session, listening to parts of two debates—one on the topic of local democracy and a second on global warming. While the content of the global warming debate was particularly interesting to students, given then-President Bush's rather controversial position that there was not enough scientific evidence to blame human activities for global warming, as well as the U.S.'s refusal to ratify the Kyoto Protocol, the sessions were also enlightening from a different perspective: they allowed students to experience first-hand the multilingual debates that are so commonplace in Europe and which I had hopelessly attempted to describe back home. In short, these and other such educational experiences that became the focus of many of my students' post-trip writing assignments revealed to me that most of them had learned a great deal from our European adventure — and indeed had a great time after all.

But what about the other students — those who had the greatest cultural "difficulties" in Europe — the ones for whom I had assumed the course had been a failure? Did I learn anything from them? And did they get anything of value from this study abroad course?

Remarkably, this second group of students contributed the most valuable lesson: that important, indeed transformative, learning can often occur when individuals experience discomfort, difficult circumstances, and challenges, when they suddenly find themselves in situations that challenge their world views and belief systems. While students experiencing such learning may not say what instructors love to hear — "This was the best course of my college years" — and while they may not even fully realize the value of the course until long after it has been completed, a valuable lesson may indeed be learned. Take, for example, what one rather difficult student wrote about his homestay in one assignment: "Our experience has helped us understand that, although separated by a large body of water, Europeans and Americans are quite similar: we are all people, with our strengths and weaknesses. Our European home has helped destroy our original ideal of Europeans and made us leery of believing stereotypes in the future."

And on a different topic,

> [Prior to departure,] I believed, [t]he food would be fabulous, the people friendly and happy, houses and monuments would sparkle in the sunshine, and I would enjoy it all as I strolled down the clean streets [of Europe]. . . . When I arrived . . . it was raining and cold. While on the trip if asked what I would have changed, I could have named a

hundred things. But now, looking back, I would have to say nothing. For without those experiences, which at the time seemed very unpleasant, I would still be carrying around my unrealistic view of Europe. This original picture was perfect but untouchable and therefore also not relatable. Europe is still a beautiful place ... but it's not perfect, which really just makes it more interesting and exciting to visit.

Thus, through the eyes of these most "difficult" students, I learned a most valuable pedagogical lesson: if these students learned to understand — even value — the cultural and other differences they faced in Europe, if they returned home cognizant of the stereotyping they had engaged in prior to departure, and if they came to view stereotypical images of others as artificial and false, then study abroad — as challenging as it can be at times — is indeed a culturally-enriching, eye-opening experience and one that, despite my initial reaction, I plan to make available to future groups of students.

CHAPTER THREE

The F-Word: The Challenges and Rewards of Facilitating Difficult Conversations

Elizabeth A. Bennion

Long hair?
Check.

Make-up?
Check.

Modest dress?
Check.

Fitted blazer?
Check.

High-heel boots?
Check.

Tasteful jewelry?
Check.

Wedding ring?
Check.

I made a mental checklist as I dressed for the first day of a new semester. Because I was teaching a new course on feminism, I wore an outfit that made me feel both powerful and feminine. Professional, but non-threatening. I was mid-way into my thirteenth year of full-time teaching, but I had never taken on a course quite like this before. The course title—"The F-Word: Historical and Contemporary Debates about Feminism"—foreshadowed the controversial nature of the course. If students expected a butch, free-love lesbian, I would present a femme, married heterosexual. If students expected a radical who dressed in defiance of conventional gender norms, I would dress conservatively, in keeping with convention. I would comfort the most skeptical students with my appearance, ensure that they did not drop the course, and help them to "identify" with me, before challenging them to think deeply about the world around them, to challenge conventional wisdom, and see the socially-constructed dimension of "natural" gender roles.[1]

The goal of this course was not to turn conservatives into liberals, traditionalists into radicals; not to make men more feminine or women more masculine; not to argue that stay-at-home moms are betraying feminism, nor that they are required for the betterment of society. Rather, the goal was to get students to understand the choices they make, that these choices might have social or political ramifications, and how such choices are constrained by social expectations, laws, and norms. The goal was to get students to challenge

---

1. See Betsy Lucal's discussion of the implications of living in a gender system that recognizes "two and only two" genders and the consequences of such a system for individuals whose "gender displays" are deemed "inappropriate." Lucal, Betsy. "What It Means to Be Gendered Me: Life on the Boundaries of a Dichotomous Gender System." *Gender and Society*, Vol. 13, No. 6 (Dec., 1999), pp. 781-797, accessed at http://www.jstor.org/stable/190440. The article discusses Lucal's experiences as a woman whose appearance often leads to gender misattribution and offers a critique of Lorber's assertion that "gender bending" serves to perpetuate, rather than break down, gender categories.

their own beliefs, to think critically about what they believe and why, and to respect the fact that others have different life circumstances, interests, and values — and that individuals in a liberal democracy must be free to make their own decisions and to use their own talents and skills to advance as individuals, uninhibited by artificial legal or social barriers based on gender or other identity categories.

My goal as the instructor was to provide a new framework for problem-solving while inspiring critical thinking, personal reflection, creativity, curiosity, and a concern with ethical issues that students face in their everyday lives. This was a tall order. The conversations would be challenging, perhaps uncomfortable, intense. Recognizing this, I set out to assuage students' fears, to counter their stereotypes, and to welcome them into a semester-long conversation. What follows is a discussion of lessons I learned through this conversation with my students.

Moderating Difficult Discussions: The Importance of Taking Risks in the Classroom

Despite fourteen years of teaching and numerous teaching awards, every semester I worry that I will fall short in the classroom — that students will not respond well to my teaching, be inspired to push themselves out of their comfort zones, deeply engage the course material, interact positively with their fellow students, or recognize what they have learned. My confidence grows each semester, and my love for teaching is renewed, when students grapple with new ideas, share insights with their peers, and engage the material critically through original analysis and synthesis.

In the "F-Word" classroom, there were several common pitfalls that I needed to avoid. Because of the subject matter of the course, avoiding them seemed more important, and more potentially difficult, than ever. Students' beliefs about gender norms are learned early and can be very rigid. Students (and teachers) have a hard time learning things that contradict their current understandings of the world; most of us filter or interpret new information we receive to confirm our earlier beliefs, theories, interpretations, and arguments (Bain, 2004; Bowen 2012). Gender identity, gender norms, and gender role expectations are certainly part of most people's understandings of themselves and the world in which they live. This is one reason the word "feminism" itself elicits strong emotional reactions.

Although some instructors share their perspectives with students while telling students that they are free to disagree, I have always chosen to introduce multiple perspectives on each issue and to let students derive their own conclusions. Over the past several years, my goal in every class has been to encourage deep learning by requiring students to think for themselves through challenging preconceived notions about the way the world works. By introducing multiple perspectives, challenging students' existing beliefs, and requiring students to point out both strengths and weaknesses of arguments on both sides of a controversial policy debate, I encourage students to move from an absolutist perspective to an evaluative one.

Students in my political controversies class routinely comment on how "unbiased" and "fair" I am in facilitating discussion and debate on controversial issues, including the death penalty, gun control, immigration reform, Muslim profiling, and torture as an interrogation technique. The controversies class has given me ample opportunity to practice the role of educator and facilitator, rather than ideologue or pundit. My goal in that class is always to get students to understand multiple perspectives and to be able to fairly articulate arguments on both (or multiple) sides of each debate, before developing a cogent, evidence-based argument supporting their own positions. The controversies class has always gotten rave reviews from students and generated many outstanding intellectually sophisticated final essays, so I knew it was possible to lead students with different ideological and partisan backgrounds in discussions of controversial topics.

And yet, I had been avoiding teaching the racial politics course for the past five years after a single student continued to argue that white males are the only people in the United States who face discrimination. No studies, statistics, or personal narratives would convince this student to give up—or to complicate—his understanding of racial politics and prejudice in the United States. My inability to break through to this student was so devastating to me that I had avoided the course ever since. Now, I was planning to challenge students' deeply held conceptions about gender and gender roles. Dare I do it? Would the students charge me with being a "FemiNazi" blinded by ideological zeal?

Lesson 1: Acknowledge Stereotypes

I dealt with the challenge of tackling controversial issues the only way I know how: by acknowledging that we would not all agree, by using disagreement to discuss the power of socialization and competing worldviews, and by stressing that there are no easy answers to many of the dilemmas we investigate. I provided a respectful space for dialogue where students could explore, and even appreciate, why people might disagree. It's often easier to discuss stereotypes when talking in general—or about others' views—rather than admitting to our own preconceptions and biases. I started by requiring students to interview people—six people, both male and female, from at least two generations and at least two different ethnic groups—asking what the term "feminist" meant to them. This provided a comfortable way to discuss the diverse understandings—both positive and negative—without requiring students to claim any particular description or viewpoint as their own. In interview results written on the board, students saw phrases like: "wants equality," "respects human rights," and "fights for civil rights" written next to phrases like "hates men," "thinks women are superior," and "refuses to shave." Why dance around the stereotypes when we can get them out in the open? Students felt free to shout out new stereotypes—especially when they did not have to claim them as their own. By speaking the "f-word" aloud, and considering a full range of diverse reactions, we were able to examine the source of such stereotypes and ask why the term elicits such powerful, and varied, emotional responses, for us and those around us.

Lesson 2: Discuss Competing Worldviews

One of the most difficult things for any educator to do is to get students to examine their own worldviews. Like political ideology, a person's worldview is a product of socialization and experience. Early childhood socialization shapes people's understanding of the way the world works and their own role in the world. These values, beliefs, and assumptions about the way the world works—and the way it should work—are reinforced (or challenged) through other agents of socialization, including schools, peers, workplaces, and media. Such agents of socialization are powerful, in part, because they remain largely invisible to those being socialized.

Learning about gender role expectations is part of the socialization process for boys and girls in all cultures. Even students who support gender equality and reject rigid gender roles in principle seldom interrogate their own expectations regarding dating, marital roles, or childcare. They may reject the notion of "men's work" versus "women's work" but, when asked about specific sectors, such as military service, they return to essentialist notions about the "proper" role of men and women in society or to "natural" or "biological" differences that necessitate different roles and responsibilities. They generalize based on their own experiences, but struggle to consider that others may have different opportunities and experiences that shape both the availability and nature of their choices.

Lesson 3: Learn from the Past

Exploring history is one way to help students to understand the power of shifting cultural attitudes and to help them to recognize their own assumptions and worldviews. The F-Word course traces the roots of feminism, including the *first-wave* struggle for voting rights (1860-1920), the *second wave* women's rights movement in the 1960–70s, and the diverse and diffuse *third wave* movement from the 1980s to the present. The course focuses on reoccurring and emerging controversies regarding the nature of women's rights and what it means to be a feminist. Students read famous texts that launched the women's rights movement and learn about key feminist victories (constitutional amendments, legislation, and court rulings) as well as counter-mobilization and victories by anti-feminists (often women) who successfully defeated key feminist goals, including the Equal Rights Amendment.

When discussing gender roles and gender differences, the challenge is to get students to "see" the *socially-constructed* nature of what seems simply natural. Students must grapple with new ideas and information and construct (or reconstruct) their own understanding of the role of sex, gender, and gender roles in society. Historical primary source documents, including books, articles, photographs, and video footage, are helpful because they allow students to "see" for themselves constructions of gender that appear strange — or downright immoral — from their own worldview as men and women living in 21ˢᵗ-century America. Similarly, a discussion of contemporary women in other nations (such as Saudi Arabia) can help students "see" the power of gender in defining social boundaries, roles, and power relations. Recognizing that women in our own country faced legal restrictions on voting, property ownership, and entry into the professions, as well as strong social norms against driving, playing sports, or speaking in churches, helps students to understand that gender roles are not "natural" and gender equality is not an automatic byproduct of democracy. Learning about the long history of struggle, protest, and violent backlash helps students to understand that women's rights are not inevitably tied to economic development. Rather, ordinary citizens must fight for human rights and equality. This is true worldwide, whether in North America or the Middle East.

Lesson 4: Get Emotional

Recent studies of the human brain suggest that the "best and most lasting learning is motivated by emotion and solidified by practice" (Bowen, 2012, p. 78). Films, video clips, and primary source documents can help students to connect with the material on both an intellectual and emotional level, making it more likely that students will retain and internalize what they have learned. Students report learning a great deal about the suffrage movement from watching the movie *Iron Jawed Angels*, despite the fact that they are required to read about the movement, learn key facts about the movement, and view a PowerPoint presentation highlighting key political actors depicted in the film before watching the movie. By combining a powerful historical narrative with a strong script, superb acting, dramatic music, and on-screen depictions of brutality and courage, the film makes it possible for viewers to connect with the characters on an emotional level, making it a lesson they are unlikely to forget. Indeed, numerous alumni from my gender politics course have told me that they have hosted their own screenings of the film because it had such a profound impact on their lives — including their own participation in the electoral process. Learning history in a way that allows students to connect on an emotional level with the narrative — or to imagine themselves there — helps students to internalize and retain what they have learned. The "F-Word" course was an excellent opportunity to put this advice into practice.

Lesson 5: Make It Personal

"The F-Word: Historical and Contemporary Controversies about Feminism" — the title was a play on words notating the fact that many students view feminism as taboo. "I'm not a feminist, but . . ." is, perhaps, the most common phrase uttered in an introductory women's studies course and in other courses discussing gender roles and gender equality. Students, though supportive of gender equality in the workplace and beyond, remain unlikely to identify themselves as feminists and shy away from questioning the ways that gender shapes their own lives, beliefs, and expectations of themselves and others.

Students were required to complete a series of reflective assignments, including one in which they reflected on their own sex, gender identity, and sexual orientation based upon new understandings of the differences (and connections) between biological sex, gender identity, sexuality, and gender roles. Students were required to describe ways that they "perform" their gender (e.g., dress, make-up, hairstyle, posture) as well as ways that they defy conventional gender-based cultural norms (e.g., going into a non-traditional profession, enjoying a hobby or exhibiting a behavior generally "reserved" for the other gender). Students were surprised by the degree to which their everyday "choices" are shaped, in part, by their own unconscious or conscious attempts to perform their gender. They also began to discuss stereotypes they held — sometimes unconsciously — about people who do not exhibit conventional gender identity markers or "appropriately perform" their expected gender roles.

Similarly, students were required to complete an online "Am I a Feminist?" quiz and to provide feedback on at least three questions — items that they found particularly important, problematic, or thought-provoking. This led students to examine their own assumptions and behaviors in some surprising ways. For example, one newly dating couple in the class learned that the woman in the relationship expected that her boyfriends would always pay for dates, including meals and concert tickets. In contrast, her boyfriend admitted that he did not really believe that he should have to pay for everything just because he has a Y chromosome. He argued that she was actually better off financially than he was and suggested that it would be nice if she offered to pay, or to share the cost, from time to time. Other students admitted that they hadn't thought about the implications of a situation in which men are expected to pay for dates, while still others bemoaned the pressure for (or expectation of) sexual favors they felt when one person was footing the bill. This discussion led to a broader discourse about whether "chivalry" is compatible with gender equality and whether equal rights require equal obligations.

Lesson 6: Highlight Complexity

The goal of the feminism course, similar to the goal of most of my courses, is to get students to think deeply and critically about the world in which they live. This course is not designed to convey "answers" and does not reward students for providing the "right" answers. Rather, course materials, assignments, and discussions are designed to promote critical thinking. The goal is to get students to use a new lens — a feminist lens — to ask new questions. Students are not expected to agree on the answers to these questions. Rather, they are expected to recognize why these questions are important, why members of our society might disagree on the answers, what is at stake in answering these questions, and how their own answers are shaped by their socialization, life experiences, and worldview. What does it mean to say that one is a "feminist"? Is there room for everyone under the feminist umbrella? Can both Hillary Clinton and Sarah Palin claim the designation, or has the term itself become meaningless?

Lesson 7: Disagree with Respect

Students must be encouraged to welcome diverse viewpoints and to discuss difficult issues with respect. During the first week of class, I noticed that some of my more liberal female students were getting impatient and frustrated with a more conservative male student in the class. For example, this student challenged the argument that women should not be relegated to the role of homemakers, stressing the importance of that work to society. While several students seemed ready to engage in verbal combat with this student, I thanked him for his reflections and stressed the important insight that caregiving has been devalued in our society. I noted the fact that feminist theorists (and activists) have discussed the importance of valuing the work that women do inside the home — while not assuming that all women, or only women, should be homemakers. This opened up a valuable discussion.

Students in the course identified with different political parties and placed themselves at different points along the left-right ideological continuum. They disagreed on specific policy proposals and shared no uniform "feminist" identification. And, yet, they listened, they learned, they respected each other, and they came away with a new understanding of the way that gender shapes individuals and societies and an enhanced appreciation of the importance of ordinary citizens in bringing about social change.

Lesson 8: Let Students Teach

Part of creating a student-centered learning environment is encouraging students to frame the conversation, take ownership of their learning, and contribute their own knowledge and skills in ways that help others learn. Throughout the semester, students in the F-Word course were encouraged to access contemporary blogs, memes, news stories, music, and YouTube videos about women's rights. As tech-natives, students are in a unique position to use new media to explore and introduce competing worldviews. During the semester I was teaching the course, Soomo Press produced a music video set to the tune of Lady Gaga's song "Bad Romance" and depicting critical events from *Iron Jawed Angels*, the suffrage film we watched together as a class. Also that semester, two independent musicians calling themselves the "Reformed Whores" produced a video entitled *I'm a Slut* to protest Rush Limbaugh's comments about Sandra Fluke, a law school student who testified in favor of the Affordable Care Act's contraception mandate.[2] Both of these video resources were suggested by students in the class who saw them on Facebook. These student-suggested videos entertained the students, but they also got them excited, because they were able to *understand* them in a way that they could not have understood them before taking the class. Students in the class did not share a uniform opinion on the contraception mandate, but they all

---

2. The title of the music group and song make it unlikely that I would have sought out or played this song in class of my own volition. As it turns out, the duo and the song are both PG material.

gained a new understanding of the complexity of the issue and a better understanding of why Americans disagree on critical policy debates. Moreover, they were excited to be able to explain the background behind each video to their social media friends. They were ready and eager to share what they were learning with others beyond the classroom. This, of course, is a college teacher's dream!

Lesson 9: Stop Being the "Expert"

When moderating difficult discussions, the instructor should foster a student-centered and learning-centered classroom. This does not mean that the instructor does not need a solid command of the field, nor does it mean that all answers are equally correct. Rather, giving up the role of expert requires recognizing the unique perspectives, life experiences, and disciplinary or professional backgrounds that students bring to the conversation. For the feminism course, I moved away from textbooks and pre-assigned weekly academic readings. Instead, I continually updated the assignment schedule on a weekly basis to allow student input, newly published materials, and contemporary debates to become part of our collective reading and learning experience. The specific assignments were created week-by-week to reflect current political discourse and debates. I played the role of facilitator, providing some historical background and theoretical frameworks that students could use to educate themselves and each other. "We're all in this together." "We all bring unique perspectives to the table." I said this, but I also felt it and lived it along with the students. I reflected on how the theories we discussed applied to my life and asked the students to do the same. Positive results were not assured, but positive results followed. As one student put it in the course evaluation: "This course is one that has taught me a lot, especially about myself. I am very satisfied with my choice in attending this class. I will take everything that I learned with me on my journey through life."

Lesson 10: Keep Them Guessing

As the opening checklist demonstrates, I consciously challenged students' assumptions about what a feminist instructor would look like, act like, think, say, and believe. While discussing the critique of marriage, I wore my wedding ring and mentioned my husband, wedding, and in-laws. While noting the unequal workload that men and women assume in the home, I noted that my husband does most of the housework in our family. While reading about the dangers faced by stay-at-home mothers, I admitted to enjoying the benefits of a stay-at-home mother growing up and to adopting the stay-at-home parent (stay-at-home dad) model as an adult. While considering the role of the Church in women's subjugation, I mentioned my family's regular attendance at religious services. The goal was not to turn attention to my own life or to suggest that I had the "answers" to the dilemmas we discussed. Instead, the goal was to illustrate the complexities of these issues and to reinforce the notion that people make a wide variety of decisions — and should be free to do so — while taking care not to stereotype others or limit their ability to achieve their full potential. I think that my own willingness to share some information about the role of gender expectations in my own life made students more comfortable reflecting on their lives. For example, one African-American woman in the course admitted that she would prefer to stay at home with her children, but that this was no more feasible for her than it had been for her own mother. A few white women in the class spoke up to indicate that this model never fit their family either. This led to an interesting discussion about the ways in which the image of the Cleaver Family never reflected the reality of people's lives across racial, ethnic, and economic categories. Additional students began to chime in to discuss their belief that the stay-at-home parent model is bad for the parent staying home because of the degree of financial risk it places him or her in, while others expressed a strong preference to work outside of the home. Still others referred to recent news stories about the "unfair" tax benefits given to married couples in households with a single wage earner. Because I reflected an openness to all viewpoints and pointed out the complexity of the issues we were discussing through my choice of readings, the questions I asked, and the critiques I raised about social conventions — sometimes matching my own life choices — I created a comfortable environment in which all perspectives were welcomed and valued. As one student put it in a course evaluation, "Normally, I don't like to get into discussions when talking about this issue, but Professor Bennion did not make it awkward in any way, and allowed everyone to express themselves and their opinions willingly."

Facilitating Difficult Discussions: Worth the Risk

My experience teaching the F-Word class for the first time highlighted the fact that challenging students' personal beliefs pushes students to develop higher-level cognitive skills, including the negotiation of meaning, the connection of information across disciplines, teamwork, and reflection on the significance of content (see Bowen, 2012, p. 21, for a more complete list of recommendations). Teaching in ways that challenges students' deeply-held, often unexamined, beliefs is inherently risky. Virtually every theory of learning predicts resistance when core beliefs or principles are challenged. And yet, without taking this risk, we compromise our ability to teach and students' ability to learn.

My fears about students disliking the course, the instructor, and the topic were not realized. Despite the controversial nature of the topics we discussed, students were uniformly positive in their anonymous evaluations of the course, indicating that they would recommend both the instructor and the course to their friends. Students answered these questions enthusiastically saying: "Yes, yes, yes," "Definitely," "Absolutely," "Without a doubt," and "I would take it again if I could." But the ultimate goal of an educator is not popularity.

The goal of a college teacher is to "reach" students intellectually, but also to leave them wanting more (Bowen, 2012, p.7). For me, the best affirmation of my work in this course came three months after the class had ended. A young man called me at the office and informed me that he had been meaning to call me for several weeks. He told me that my class had changed the way he thought about the world. The same student who argued forcefully during the first week of class that a man is a failure *as a man* if he is not the primary breadwinner for his family,[3] now told me that he continued to use the frameworks and knowledge he learned in the course every day. He relayed discussions and debates that he had been having around the dinner table with his traditional Italian ("machismo-promoting") uncles. He thanked me for changing his outlook, freeing him from narrow gender-based conceptions of success and failure, and expanding his worldview. This student felt extremely nervous after signing up for a course about "women's liberation" — but found, in the end, that it was *he* who was liberated. He felt more able to explore his interest in nursing and more able to envision a variety of ways in which he might fulfill the role of husband and father later in life. He was relieved to be able to consider a wide range of choices that he had never realized were possible. This student thanked me for a

---

3. This is not the same (conservative male) student referred to earlier in the chapter.

transformative experience. Teaching this course was worth the risk a thousand times over, because no educator can ask for more than that.

References

Bain, K. (2004). *What the Best College Teachers Do.* Cambridge, MA: Harvard University Press.

Bowen, J. A. (2012). *Teaching Naked: How Moving Technology Out of Your College Classroom Will Improve Student Learning.* San Francisco, CA: Jossey-Bass.

Lucal, B. (1999). What It Means to Be Gendered Me: Life on the Boundaries of a Dichotomous Gender System. *Gender and Society,* 13 (6), 781-797.

CHAPTER FOUR

Teaching in Circles

Vince Peterson

My formal teaching experience began as a middle school social studies student teacher. It was in a typical school and a regular classroom in Champaign, Illinois. I had an excellent critic teacher who had great rapport with his students. I quickly learned the protocol of being on the other side of the desk. I learned how helpful it is to be tuned in to individual students and their possible issues — and not just to stay there.

My first paying job as a teacher began in 1960 as a Social Studies teacher at a high school in Calumet City, Illinois. Here I taught mainly courses in Civics/American Government, Geography, Economics, and American Problems. Again, it was a typical classroom building with all the seats carefully aligned in rows — but at least the seats were not bolted to the floor, as some desks were in older buildings.

The flexibility in seating arrangements became important, because as my teaching career continued, I found myself adopting more of a minister's approach to subject matter. I would hold any lecture sessions to an average of 20 minutes or so, spending the remainder of the session in classroom interaction — an actual "social" studies approach to working with the various topics.

The student desk formation became very important in this setup, because for the ultimate in social interaction in a classroom, perhaps the best arrangement is a circle. Since this type of configuration is not always possible because of room and class size, I had students arrange their desks in a "U" formation, where I would at least begin the session at the top of the "U." (If a class was very large, I would try to set up the room with a "double U" formation, with a second row of desks within the outside row.)

This arrangement, besides increasing the amount of student-to-student interaction in a most desirable way, also provided me with greater space in which to maneuver down the center of the "U" or all around the outside. And, most important, the students were highly approving of this setup. They relished the idea of speaking directly to another student as opposed to talking to the back of a fellow classmate's head.

After six years of teaching at the high school level, and acquiring a Master's degree along the way, I went back to the University of Illinois to get a PhD in Counseling Psychology with a minor in Educational Psychology. In 1969, I was hired at the relatively new Indiana University South Bend campus, primarily as an Educational Psychology instructor. In addition, I taught a Counseling course or two. (The Indiana University South Bend campus was so new that there was no fully developed counseling program.)

I experimented with the seating arrangements and my class presentation styles in teaching my classes when I started at Indiana University South Bend. I found that the class sizes for the most part weren't all that large, and the classrooms that I was assigned to were fairly big. So, my previous arrangement of a "U" shape configuration quickly morphed into a total circle. And while there always was an opening for me as an instructor to use a podium for a formal lecture, or for a movie, I found that the circle arrangement appealed very much to the students as well as to me. Here we could talk about all types of issues and get almost full participation of all class members.

This active participation probably had a lot to do with the teaching of Educational Psychology to future teachers. It seems that almost everyone has ideas as to how best to teach elementary and secondary school students. However, I have found that this approach also works well with a wide variety of other subjects.

In most cases, I assigned readings specific to the topic of the class session. Then, as each individual's participation was evaluated, it generally became evident whether or not various students had come prepared.

I also taught graduate level courses. I actually finished my career at Indiana University South Bend teaching only graduate courses in the Counseling and Human Services Program. I used the same circle format in these courses. In fact, I found the circular arrangement was perhaps most fitting at this level. Motivation was higher at this level and the students had much more life experience; therefore, participation was even greater than at the lower levels. As a result, I got to know each of the students and their abilities fairly quickly.

One of the desirable aspects of the circular arrangement is the fact that it leads easily into other variations. I could quickly have the students arrange themselves into dyads, triads, etc., when a given topic lent itself to smaller group participation. This small group participation was also a great asset as it more directly involved all of the students in a given topic.

Many other courses are already set up for variations of this approach, such as all laboratory courses. Also, practicum and internship courses often use this approach.

Vince Peterson passed away at the age of 76, before he could finish this essay. Joy Alexander wrote the following essay in his honor.

Homage to a Colleague, Mentor, and Friend

Jannette (Joy) Alexander

I am privileged to have known Vince Peterson, a beloved colleague, mentor, and friend. I was fortunate to work with Vince and to learn from him for the first 15 years of my professional career at Indiana University South Bend.

Vince had written a short essay for this book but was not able to see it through publication. This essay pays tribute to Vince, his teaching/counseling legacy, his impact on my teaching, and his influence on his students. In this essay, I provide examples of Vince's pedagogy and practice, discuss how his instructional strategies have influenced my own teaching, and discuss how his students regard him as both a teacher and counselor.

Vince was a major player in establishing the Counseling and Human Services graduate program at Indiana University South Bend almost four decades ago. He was indefatigable and steadfast in his effort to make the program one of the finest in the state. Vince was also quite instrumental in the establishment of Indiana University South Bend's University Center for Excellence in Teaching (UCET).

Vince was revered by both faculty and students. He was well-known on campus and in surrounding communities. His active listening ear, his large intellect, and his warm sense of humor drew both students and professionals into his circle of affiliation. Their lives were touched and forever changed by his counsel and by his example.

His influence extended beyond the borders of Indiana University South Bend. For example, he was an evaluator for the Council for Accreditation of Counseling and Related Educational Programs (CACREP) where he visited campuses throughout the country. He also wrote a comprehensive textbook on counseling used by faculty members throughout the country for many years.

Vince was a man of tall stature with a quiet wisdom and patience about him. One of his students remarked that he was really taller than his actual height because he stood above others in the inviting and deep attention that he gave to all people unconditionally. His unhurried approach, his warmth and kindness inspired confidence in those with whom he interacted, and his patient attention invited all to share the things that were most important to them with him.

When I received my doctoral degree, Vince was ready and available to help me in my journey to become a seasoned academician and an effective helper/healer. As a doctoral student, I was used to being given practical feedback along the lines of "this is what you do to be successful." I was hoping that Vince would be as prescriptive, but his mentoring and teaching style turned out to be the exact opposite. He encouraged and allowed me to find my own way and was more inclined to speak very little about the dos and don'ts that I wanted to hear. Though our styles of teaching and counseling were very different, I find myself in retrospect both admiring and acknowledging the influence of Vince's humanistic, "unconditional positive regard" stance. For him, it was not just a counseling practice. It was how he saw and interacted with the world.

If I were to summarize Vince's teaching style, it would be "existential humanistic" (EH), utilizing many of the same techniques and approaches with his students that Carl Rogers utilized in his Rogerian counseling with his clients. Vince fully embraced the existential humanistic theory of counseling and modeled the best of its principles in his teaching. He deeply believed in the uniqueness of each individual and the importance of each individual's voice and perspective. He encouraged students to explore their experiences and find their own meaning in each encounter they had. He emphasized the idea that individuals use their own values to determine personal choice, thus resulting in personal responsibility for any and all of their choices. In the EH theory, responsibility and choice work together with the notion that, ultimately, we are alone in this world and how we deal with our feelings of aloneness helps us arrive at the meaning we ascribe to our existence. Then out of the choices that follow, outcomes would be positive or negative.

Vince created well-appointed scenarios and activities in class that heightened the students' awareness of their aloneness. His genius bloomed in his mastery of conveying as a counselor the assurance of his being with each student while he or she stood in his or her aloneness. One student, remembering one of these exercises, remarked, "He was justice incarnate to all. With acceptance and sensitivity, he could sort through the most difficult of issues, leaving us with our spirits intact. He always had forgiving eyes. I could always sob and cry in his presence and leave with my dignity still intact." What an amazing legacy!

When I asked Vince to observe my class, I was hoping that he would provide me with definitive suggestions to better my craft. He did not. Instead, he asked me questions — "How do you think you performed? What was the best part of what you did today?

How might you do things differently if you were to have another attempt at teaching this subject matter again?" Pleadings to him to get a response to "How did I do?" would be met with "How do you think you did?" This was so frustrating for me, but it also allowed me to fully focus on my own definition of success and self-reliance. This was foundational to Vince's approach to learning and healing. It was the fruit of his life philosophy, experienced by others, which drew people to Vince and caused them to both love and admire him.

There was a time on campus when Vince's students could be easily spotted by their constant repetition in their conversation of the phrase, "I am . . ., and I take responsibility for it." Students would appear in my class making such statements as "I am tired, and I take responsibility for my tiredness." "I am angry, and I take full responsibility for my anger." "I am feeling hopeful, and I take full responsibility for my hope." The practice of repeating the "responsibility mantra" became contagious, and for a while, we all were "taking responsibility" for anything and everything we were aware of. This was healthy for us and for others in our lives. There were no "victims" in Vince's estimation.

With less emphasis on lecturing, Vince' s classes were never dull but full of discussions and experimentation with ideas and techniques. His students attested to their admiration of his low key, humble style that made him admit to not always knowing or being the expert. He graciously entertained student opinions different from his own; he admitted his frustrations with certain aspects of practicing as a counselor. And, of course, the greatest emphasis in his classes was the EH practice of being in the here-and-now. Some students, acquainted with Vince's classes, would refer to them as "here-and-now." "I am going to 'here-and-now' in a few minutes." They would say, "Do we actually have 'here-and-now' assignments due today?" Living and experiencing the present moment (now referred to in some circles as the practice of mindfulness) is what made Vince's classes full of life and vibrancy. Students regularly reported that the CHS program was three years of therapy, and that Vince's class, in particular, was "intense therapy." They mentioned living in the here-and-now, being with their anxiety, and making their personal meaning of it all.

This, then, was the brilliance of Vince's teaching: taking the elements of being human that the students brought into his classroom and using this human vulnerability as his instrument of imparting the principles of empowerment and responsibility he wished to establish in them.

When I observed Vince in the classroom, he was in his element. It was in these classroom observations where he usually had students seated together in a circle that I began to understand the effectiveness of his EH approach to teaching. I never saw students bored or overwhelmed in his class, even though it was three hours long. That was a testament to the kind of teacher that he was.

They say life is therapy. While I agree, I also say teaching is therapy. Vince used the EH approach as a therapeutic framework to teach his students about life and how they can approach their clients' lives in a therapeutic setting. While I started out questioning Vince's approach, I realized that teaching using the EH framework was quite effective, as I witnessed during the classroom visits that I had with him and his students and later in my own teaching.

I am proud to say that, armed with the EH approach and others that I have learned through the years from Vince, my teaching has evolved. I have a therapeutic approach to teaching in much the same way that Vince did.

Over the years, I have come to appreciate Vince's methods even more and have taken what I learned from him further than he would have anticipated. For the past several years, my teaching has emphasized personal and environmental context over the content of the course. Like Vince, I fully embrace the principle of offering unconditional positive regard (UPR) to my students and I embrace Carl Rogers' principle that providing a safe and nurturing space for students to learn will give them the freedom they need to develop in the way that their instinct and soul allow — all within the permeable margins of the course syllabus. Their individual growth must be of primary consideration in addition to the academics of the course.

One of the Vince-inspired methods that I have found to be very effective in my teaching is to have the students develop their own system of self-evaluation. This was accomplished by instituting certain requirements in my courses. As part of my course learning outcomes, students were required to develop their personal goals for what they hoped to learn in the course. They were further required to develop the standard by which they would be evaluated to ascertain their achievement of those goals. Finally, they were required to evaluate their performance over the semester and suggest the grade they thought they earned, based on their own standards.

This was usually disconcerting to new students who were not acquainted with this method, but by the end of the semester, they usually attested to their increased self-awareness, self-confidence, and self-efficacy. This practice of self-evaluation was consistent throughout my interactions with students during the semester activities. I tried to emulate Vince's practice of offering minimal praise or criticism. I strove to invite students to evaluate their own performance, develop the habit of self-reflection, and learn to apply their own praise and affirmations of their progress. They also became adept at identifying the areas in their skill set that they could choose to enhance. My standard response to student requests for feedback was an echoing of Vince's questions — "what might happen if . . . ?"

I believe, however, that my methods and practices would not have succeeded outside of the context of a very supportive atmosphere in the classroom. I was fortunate enough to discover the power of such never-failing rituals in my classroom as having my students recite to themselves their own "taking responsibility" mantras. We always started our class with a centering exercise where students learned the relaxation techniques of behavior therapy, applied them to their own lives, and got them to join the bodies they brought into the classroom. If I forgot to lead the class in this ritual, students would remind me. I believe that such rituals served to lend predictability and grounding for the students and afforded them the security of doing the radical explorations in which we engaged.

As a counselor, I was always aware of the energy in my classroom and sought to maintain the optimum excitement with just enough tension to motivate but not stress the students. Vince would have been proud of these attempts to use existential anxiety to teach the counseling principles! My usual method of accomplishing this excitement and "therapeutic anxiety" was through exercises that allowed them instant achievement and satisfaction as they strove to grapple with other concepts that required more time to grasp and implement. Again, context mattered more than the content in my lesson design.

In tandem with the requirement for self-awareness and self-evaluation, another "Vince-inspired" central feature of my teaching is to have students use the counseling principles being explored to address a challenge they identify in their lives during that semester. The goal of the assignment is not so much to resolve the challenge but for students to constantly review their efforts and to have them evaluate their reactions to the results of their efforts. Students who are keenly aware of their struggles and triumphs as well as the factors influencing their outcomes usually report more self-growth and display a deeper grasp of the principles that were studied. This vintage Peterson method has been a source of great advancement for my students.

One of the most basic and truly profound principles of counseling is the gift of true listening. This principle was well-utilized in Vince's classes and a source of healing and growth for students in my own classes. By design, students were required to engage in many partnerships to complete assignments and to reflect on their experiences of being seen and heard by their colleagues. They were to describe the effect this had on them. Vince took these principles to a higher level by giving substantial credit to those students who completed a semester of practicum or internship in counseling without asking the question "why?" Students became more skilled in moving from the reason for a circumstance or phenomenon to the solutions and choices surrounding the circumstance. This method inspired the following comment from a former student:

> I fell in love with group therapy after taking his
> class. He was an orchestra conductor, bringing
> out the melodies of the group members, whether
> the sounds were pounding and loud like drums
> or the singing violin or the voices of the flute.
> It all became music as he moved us masterfully
> together, singing to one another rather than
> trying to outdo, outtalk, or outshine each other.

One of the principles Vince emphasized is that all counseling is grief counseling. Students report that their attempts to refute this principle always ended in their coming to believe that counseling is truly the acknowledgment of life and expectations changing and individuals having to mourn the loss created by this realization. Vince taught that sometimes it is necessary to let go of one note or one musical phrase in the symphony of life. In doing so, we create the opportunity and the capacity to appreciate change and to enjoy the full and complete meaning of the symphony.

Vince excelled at conveying these principles to his students. He created and introduced many rituals for students to move from one topic to the other, from one theory to the other, from one course to the other, and from student to counselor and colleague. His students reached their goals because, from the first day of his classes, he introduced the idea of change and letting go and acknowledging and honoring the process. He was true to the counseling principle that the counselor sets up the termination process from the first day of getting acquainted with the client. Vince's colleagues and former students now reflect his principles in their personal and professional lives, and the examined lives that they witness are more powerful and self-actualized as a result of his teaching. I have followed this process of self-examination with my students and have found similar results.

Truly, I must say that Vince Peterson practiced in his own professional and personal life the principles of self-actualization that he held so deeply. He lived to help others become the best that they could choose to be. This deeply held value was reflected not only in his teaching and his students but also in the development of the teaching center (UCET) that focused on supporting faculty to be at their best in their academic careers and as human beings. At UCET, the embodiment of what Vince believed and lived and taught can be seen.

Vince undeniably left his mark not only at Indiana University South Bend but also in the hearts of all who had the privilege of knowing him, working with him, and being with him — faculty, students, counselors — myself included. Well done, Vince. You will never be forgotten.

Note: The UCET Advisory Board named the faculty development classroom the "Peterson Classroom" in Vince's honor. The Peterson Education and Counseling Suite in the School of Education is named in honor of Vince and his wife Carolyn, as is the Peterson Scholarship in Counseling.

CHAPTER FIVE

The Passing of the Trash Can

Gwynn Mettetal

Sometimes we learn more from our failures than from our successes.

I had been teaching for quite a few years in a variety of disciplines (child development is ubiquitous) and landed in a school of education, teaching educational psychology courses. A few weeks before the fall semester began, I was asked to teach the graduate education course in Classroom Management. "You realize that I have never taught a K-12 class," I said. But the Dean was desperate, so I agreed. I found a textbook that covered several different theoretical approaches and felt reassured — these seemed to be very much like the various parenting approaches with which I was very familiar. I could do this! I found a great book of case studies and wrote a syllabus that focused on discussion and applications to those cases.

I had a full class (27 in a graduate class!) and started the semester with great enthusiasm. I was an experienced, tenured professor, and I knew my way around a classroom. Teaching has always been my strength, so I was sure that this would work out fine. To my dismay, it was soon apparent that I was wrong. The first night, students discussed the syllabus assignments briefly, asked a few questions, and seemed ready to leave. I was surprised. In my experience, classroom management is a "hot topic" for teachers. I expected them to dive into the topic with enthusiasm. Their listless response gave me pause.

Their lack of participation the second week made me even more nervous. Yes, nearly everyone had taken that week's theory and tried to apply it to the assigned case study, but their discussion was very superficial and my attempts to move them to a deeper level failed miserably. As I proceeded to introduce the next week's theory, I could tell that the class was not "with me." We finished early (not surprising, since no one asked any questions), and there was a rush for the door.

On the third week, I noticed sideways glances and rolling of eyes throughout much of the class. I was close to tears on the drive home. What was going on? Why couldn't I reach them? Had I lost my "touch" as a teacher? Was it the book? Was my lack of K-12 experience showing? Did I need better examples? Suddenly the answer hit me — most of these graduate students were experienced teachers in the field. They might not know all of the theoretical (and practical) approaches that we would discuss in class, but they certainly had experience in managing classrooms. By assigning nothing but case studies, I was not respecting the accumulated knowledge and experience of my students. I was asking them to apply knowledge to case studies, when they could apply it to their own real-life classrooms.

I went home and revised the syllabus radically. Instead of focusing the assignments and class discussions on the case studies from the book, I had them focus on their own classroom. (Only the few students who had never taught would rely on the cases.) The others would reflect each week on their own classes, and discuss what that week's theoretical approach would look like in their own classes, and how well they thought it would work in that particular situation. The major assignment of a classroom management plan would be tailored to meet each teacher's own classroom needs, rather than be an abstract theoretical exercise.

Now the big question: how could I introduce this change to the students and still maintain a shred of dignity? I thought about various rationales (really excuses) for the change. But I finally decided to go with the most honest approach, although spiced with a bit of drama and humor.

"Everyone, I need you to take out your class syllabus." I waited while they all did. "Hold it up high." Long pause while they all followed direction. "Now — tear it in two!" There were puzzled looks and glances at classmates. "Really — tear it in two," I repeated. I watched as everyone followed my instructions. "Now it is time for the ritual of the Passing of the Trash Can. When the can comes to you, throw your syllabus in!" I gave the can to the first student and watched it pass down the rows, as students nervously giggled, wondering what was coming.

"You all are so polite — no one said anything — but I could tell this class was not going well," I told them. "Yes, I have knowledge that will be useful, but you have years of experience in the classroom. I've written a new syllabus that asks you to use your *own* experiences as you complete class assignments. I printed it on yellow paper so that you would know it was a different version." I passed it out and gave them a chance to read it over. There was silence as they read, then whispers, then some smiles. "This looks good!" one of them ventured. "Yes!" said another. "This will actually be *useful!*"

After a brief explanation of how this would change their assignments, we resumed class with the "classroom management perspective of the day," which was now focused on their own classes instead of case studies. The classroom was quickly buzzing with small group discussions of how the perspective could be implemented in their own classrooms, and whether or not it would be helpful. As I expected, there were often disagreements, which were resolved when students considered the particular needs of their specific classrooms. When groups reported out, I was thrilled with the depth of their analysis of the perspective as they contemplated its implementation in a variety of actual classrooms. This was the class that I had imagined teaching, full of enthusiastic, engaged learners!

There was one more affirming event that evening. After class, a student approached me. She said, "I was so unhappy with this class that I brought a drop slip to have you sign. But this new syllabus is great! I want to stay and work on a plan for my classroom!" She dramatically tore her drop slip in two, and threw it into the trashcan. That night I drove home with a smile on my face. The rest of the semester was very successful, with lively discussions and outstanding student work, and the course evaluations were very positive.

Here are the top ten lessons I learned (or re-learned) from this experience:

1. **You need to take your students' prior experience into account.** I had asked for teaching experience on the Student Information Sheet, but forgot to think about how it would influence the class. Previous coursework is important, but life experience is, too.

2. **You need different teaching strategies for different situations.** The case study approach would have been very effective with undergrads who did not have teaching experience. Unfortunately, that is not who I was teaching.

3. **Students are more motivated when they can apply what they are learning to real situations.** When students could apply the information to their own classrooms, it became much more useful. That grabbed their attention. I was impressed with the amount of effort they put into the class over the rest of the semester. For the students who had not taught, the case studies provided a good alternative.

4. **You don't always have to be an "expert" in a content area to be a good teacher.** Helping students find their own answers is a time-honored teaching tool, and the foundation of problem-based learning. In fact, sometimes the most important lesson that you teach them might be "how to learn."

5. **Authenticity counts.** When students feel that you are being honest with them, and that you are sincerely trying to help them learn, they will usually forgive missteps.

6. **Taking risks can be a means of professional development.** Stretching yourself by teaching new courses or using new teaching strategies doesn't always go smoothly, but it keeps you fresh and helps you learn.

7. **Humor can ease the situation.** Literally passing the trash can made everyone laugh and defused some of the tension. The best situation is when you can combine humor with authenticity.

8. **We all make mistakes.** Yes, it can be embarrassing, but we all make mistakes. Since I teach Education students, I tell myself that

I am modeling how to handle those inevitable teaching missteps.

9. **Mistakes are not fatal.** It is what you *DO* about your mistake that matters. Depending on what the mistake is and how it affects students, the appropriate response may be to ignore it, to mention it briefly and move on, or to make a major change in the class.

10. **Mistakes can be a good thing.** It is easy to become complacent about your teaching. Mistakes can serve as a wake-up call to prompt us to reflect on our teaching! Through figuring out what happened and how to recover, you often take your teaching to a new level.

CHAPTER SIX

Before Dissecting, Kiss Frog

Tom Vander Ven

Before dissecting, kiss frog. That instruction, embroidered on linen in a gilt frame, was hanging on the upstairs bedroom wall of my childhood. But I didn't start brooding about it till the junior high years, during which I prepared for a robustly dysfunctional life as an adult. The instruction seemed to have something to do with royalty, maybe a princess, or advice for someone entering medical school. But I never brought it up with anyone in my family because I didn't want to seem ignorant, even though once I awoke in the night to the smell of formaldehyde. No one else ever mentioned it either. There are some things a family doesn't discuss. Twice, I took it down and stuck it in a closet, but each time it reappeared on the wall: "Before Dissecting, Kiss Frog."

No person, including me, lives life free of inconsistency and contradiction. Gaps between word and action, as well as between word and word, abound, at times astounding in their self-congratulatory flamboyance. "I'm a Christian first and a mean-spirited, bigoted conservative second, and don't you ever forget it," writes Ann Coulter, right-wing provocateur, claiming, as she sometimes does, that it's a joke. Years ago, a good friend of mine said that he could accomplish anything—with just a little extra push. So I did. Off a cliff. He was airborne for six seconds. It was a joke.

Three scenes from my early years:

Scene 1: As a boy of about ten, on the white-pillared porch of our red brick family home in Utica, Michigan, I played with a sweet, long-haired cat my mother called Tabby. She climbed on me, trustingly walking up my back as I leaned over. We fed Tabby, but my mother thought animals belonged outside. Tabby wasn't in any sense the family cat, but she was our lovable co-habitant.

Scene 2: From time to time, cats lived under that stone porch, creeping through ground level ports like miniature train tunnels that led to our basement. I built model planes at a table in that damp, stony basement—in the days before plastic toys, when we pinned thin balsa strips to a paper layout and glued the joints to form the fuselage, which we then wrapped with a translucent, fibrous paper. Once I went to the basement and found a litter of kittens on scraps of carpet in a cardboard box, hissing wildly at me. My mother told me to put the kittens into a burlap bag, tie it shut, and take the kittens to the river in a wagon. Which I did.

Scene 3: Five years later in a high school science club, our science teacher Robbie Harrison decided our nerdy club was ready to dissect a cat, so one of the guys caught a farm cat in his uncle's barn and had it put to sleep and preserved in a formaldehyde bath. We had an upscale, after-school education in examining the muscles, skeleton, and organs of that cat. One of us became an anesthesiologist, one a nurse, one a pastor, one an English professor. Another who played the flute and wanted to study art is unaccounted for. There are currently eighty-three people in Michigan named David Chapman.

I doubt that those three scenes bore any conscious, coherent relationship to each other in my boy's brain. I didn't argue with my mother about the ethics of drowning kittens. Before putting on our lab jackets and masks, we nerds didn't first hold a hearing on the right of humans to kill other species for educational purposes. We all lived in a culture that regarded cats as pets and nuisances to drown and specimens to dissect. Still, I have no recollection of anyone drowning their beloved pet cat Fluffy in order to dissect and study its anatomy. Or, for that matter, their pet frog Hopper.

I don't remember thinking how effective the human mind is at compartmentalizing its competing personal interests, and how fluently cultures balkanize values into conveniently separate domains. My mother would never have said, "Tommy, when you get done playing with Tabby, go drown those kittens." Or: "Go drown Tabby. She's a nuisance and interferes with your piano practice." Part of our skill is in maintaining functional distances between contradictory behaviors. I've done it all my life. We've done it all our lives. The tyranny of speciesism has been so profound in western culture that its behaviors have required no more decision-making than spreading peanut butter on bread.

To contradiction, add our deep well of ignorance — of the self and of the cosmos — and we have the premise for the best of comedy and tragedy. What is so dangerous about learning to say, "I don't know"? Ken Johnson at the University of Colorado told me in the '60s that the most important statement he learned to make as a graduate student in English at USC was "I don't know." It's both a strategy to survive one's oral exams and to start every day honestly. Part of the counter-argument is that the virtue of not-knowing may be a rationale for moral sloth and intellectual cowardice, which implies that genuine moral searching and intellectual study *will* lead to certainty. Just put in the hours earnestly. "Seek and ye shall find" (Matthew 7:7). But know also, know ye this, as psychologist George Miller put it, "We find what we're looking for." We find what we want to find: the mightiness of predisposition.

Careers of leadership are based on knowing, or at least on the appearance of knowing. Consider our predisposition in the academy that significant learning goes on, that teachers impart critical methodologies that lead to useful answers to important questions. Hence the tradition of the grand lecture delivered in a hall of riveted students, some of whom may have read the chapter, some of whom may be taking notes. I once passed a classroom where a professor was lecturing to what appeared to be an empty room. Making the loop around the corridor, I took another look. I had been wrong; there were two students sitting in the back row, and the professor appeared to be addressing a spot on the wall about three feet above their heads.

In the late '50s, I took a memorable undergraduate course in literary theory at the University of Michigan. Professor Norman Nelson *was* riveting—ardent, coherent, sonorous, ironic, and professorially larger than life. He didn't invite questions and apparently didn't like questions because he delivered his concluding remarks from the doorway to the hall, sometimes leaving, then re-entering for one last comment. He exited down the corridor of Angell Hall as the bell rang so no one could catch him. Had one of us died during his lecture, he would not have noticed.

Teachers can't plan their course calendars to coincide with an important historic event yet to happen in order to effect a sense of immediate, colossal relevance—the discovery of unknown biblical scrolls in a desert cave, the unearthing of a new species of hominid in East Africa, or the signing of a two-state document for Palestine and Israel. Most teachers have to muddle along the path of the ordinary semester, awakening students' imaginations to the dramatic milestones of political history or to the rich and vast cosmos in which the light of distant stars takes millions, even billions, of years to reach our retinas. The stuff of syllabi cannot wait for the announcement that there once was life on Mars or that radio telescopes have received communication transmissions from extraterrestrial life on the fourth planet of a star in Messier 32, the Andromeda galaxy.

What is the ideal course to teach that offers pedagogical certainty and energizes students with an urgency to learn? A course in the theology of End Times: "Students, we have a limited amount of time in which to position ourselves for the Final Exam, Judgment Day." History shows us that the vision of living in End Times is renewable. End Times have been repeatedly and wrongly predicted, so the agenda of the course calls for a reexamination of the data—the entrails and signs.

The late Peter Stanlis, a Robert Frost and Edmund Burke scholar, philosophical conservative, and devout Catholic, advised our mutual friend, former Indiana University South Bend Chancellor, Les Wolfson, against an agnostic stance. Stanlis called agnosticism cowardice, a lack of commitment. But Wolfson is probably the only university chancellor in history to bravely and formally address in public the virtue of negative capability: "when a man is capable of being in uncertainties, mysteries, doubts, without any irritable reaching after fact and reason" [and institutional doctrine]. Wolfson loved great music and believed it was his best means to experience the vastitude of the divine. Though yearning at times for some satisfying religious membership, he resisted formal theologies. He didn't know, but might have guessed, that of the 73 percent of the faculty who were actually listening to his address at that moment, only seven of them were English faculty, of which two remembered that they had not been able fully to explain the concept of negative capability in their own doctoral oral exams fifteen years before.

Stanlis greatly admired Frost's poetic, patriarchal wisdom as a kind of model certainty, a staunch resistance to an entropic, universal flow of being downward to nothingness. We hear this Frostian certainty in "West-Running Brook":

> Our life runs down in sending up the clock.
> The brook runs down in sending up our life.
> The sun runs down in sending up the brook.
> And there is something sending up the sun.
> It is this backward motion toward the source,
> Against the stream, that most we see ourselves in,
> The tribute of the current to the source.
> It is from this in nature we are from.
> It is most us.

We hear it in the chain of natural causes listed in reverse, in "this backward motion." And we hear it in the gravity of the syntactical repetition of the phrase, "runs down in sending," and in the stanza's final "It is . . . / It is most us." The poem pays tribute to our human urge for order, but what that order is, what that "something" is that sends up the sun, is unspecified. As is the glimpse of what — truth? — at the bottom of a well in "For Once then Something."

> What was that whiteness?
> Truth? A pebble of quartz? For
> once, then, something.

Robert Frost was himself the White Eminence of Somethingness, which he invoked in other poems as well.

> Something there is that does not love a wall.
> Choose something like a star.
> Something has to be left to God.

Stanlis found in Frost a staunch certainty of Something, but George Nitchie dismissed Frost for offering merely "a momentary stay against confusion" which, he argued, Frost's vision never fully realized. He wrote that Frost represented "the last sweepings of the Puritan latrines." Still, Frost did, in his affirmation of nature, kiss the frog, a green Frog of Somethingness.

Something like this Somethingness we find in Saul Bellow's 1976 Nobel Prize Speech: "The essence of our real condition, the complexity, the confusion, the pain of it appears to us in glimpses, in what Proust and Tolstoy thought of as 'true impressions.' This essence reveals, and then conceals itself. When it goes away it leaves us again in doubt." Intermittence. Evanescence. Something like Frost's glimpse of something, a piece of quartz, at the bottom of the well under the daylight, pieces of love, courage, fear, and wonderment.

In the classroom, we hope and strive for such glimpses, toiling in the art of embrace and the science of inquiry. Creators and analysts, syllabi in hand.

Looming over our classroom toil is the great frog of uncertainty, festooned in the many colors of our finitude. We create and analyze and lovingly rewrite the old narratives. I have always resisted the sacredness of texts, whether religious or political. Inerrancy seems to me to be errant. A chessboard on which one player's king is invisible. No checkmate possible.

Before dissecting, kiss frog. When your work is done, kiss it again.

CHAPTER SEVEN

Less Is More

Monica Maria Tetzlaff

I began my teaching career, not as a college professor, but as an elementary school teacher. My first teaching job was at Public School 150 in Brownsville, a working class neighborhood in Brooklyn. Even though I taught there for only a year because I decided to pursue a Ph.D. in history, the advice from the master teacher mentor I was assigned has helped me through many of the ups and downs of my teaching career. One thing I learned is that good teachers "steal" from other teachers. This was a humorous way of saying that it was smart to try material and methods that were working for other teachers. My mentor shared materials such as beautiful sepia-toned photographic prints of pioneering African-American women. She also taught me to draw on my strength, my love of story-telling and helping students write stories, and base my teaching on it. From that time forward, I have sometimes succeeded and sometimes failed in balancing adopting good ideas from others and teaching from my own strengths. My Freedom Summer class is one example.

Lester "Les" Lamon, my senior colleague, convinced me to teach Freedom Summer, a two-week, three-credit Civil Rights Study Tour of five southern states, by inviting me to accompany him and the class on the tour and finally by handing me a blue plastic box full of file folders with all his notes, forms, and contacts. He was retiring, and he wanted his tour to continue. It had transformed the lives of many of the students who went on it. They had gone on to form the Civil Rights Heritage Center, which, by the time I took over the class, was an active campus organization. As someone informed me (not entirely helpfully), I had "big shoes to fill."

Even though Freedom Summer was an amazing class, I was not sure it was going to work with me as the teacher. Unlike my senior colleague, I am not a supremely organized person. I enjoy running my classroom like jazz with the syllabus and readings as the score, out of which I take solo riffs, grooving off of clips of films and student questions and discussion. There is always room for improvisation. On Freedom Summer, I would have to keep to a tight schedule of appointments, meet up with speakers in relatively unfamiliar cities, and juggle many details such as hotel and lunch reservations, receipts, purchase orders, and speaker agreements. Worst of all, I could do none of this on the bus, as my predecessor had done. Reading even one or two sentences while the bus was moving could induce motion sickness.

The first time I led the trip myself, I took anti-motion sickness medicine and bravely faced backward from the direction the bus was driving, running the class while the bus zoomed down the highway. There was so little time! Our schedule was jam-packed, and I showed most of the eight-hour *Eyes on the Prize* series while we were on the bus, plus extra videos that Les had passed on to me. Each year he had run the tour he seemed to have acquired more materials and places to visit. How could I ever cover it all? Meanwhile, the students sunk lower in their seats and seemed to retreat to the back of the bus more and more while the documentaries played. The medicine kept nausea at bay, but it made me very sleepy and more than that, depressed, so that I lost the spunk and energy that usually kept me going. I had to stop taking it, even though this meant I was ill by the time we arrived at our destination.

I realized I would have to depend more on the students, and it was fortunate that Les had handed me an organized sheet of tasks from which students could choose. Instead of being the center of the classroom, I needed to see myself as the facilitator of their experience of learning. Freedom Summer forced me to rely heavily on the students as a team, and it gave them opportunities for leadership. Participation counted for 25% of their grade, and that meant faithfully fulfilling their chosen tasks, such as removing the luggage from the bus, counting to see that we were all there, or writing thank you notes to each speaker. I saw that I needed to add DVD management to the list and did. I also cut back the number of videos. I rarely lectured after we left Indiana University South Bend, where we had a full-day session preparing us for the trip. Instead, the students read prepared reports at the different sites and listened to the life stories told by local civil rights movement veterans.

Thus, I tried to keep most of the elements of Les's tour in place, but I had to somehow make it my own, playing to my strengths. In addition to going to the places Les had chosen in Alabama, Tennessee, and Mississippi, I decided to take the students to South Carolina. I'd written a book about a woman who studied the African-American "Gullah" culture of the Sea Islands of South Carolina, and I knew the islands inside and out. I had breathed the soft music of the breezes blowing the Spanish moss on the old oak trees, and I had listened with delight to the voices of the people, speaking Gullah, fishing, and singing in church. I could share my expertise and appreciation of Martin Luther King's retreat at the Penn Center and take them to experience the ocean beach at Hunting Island.

So, I added St. Helena Island, South Carolina, to the original itinerary: Memphis, Tennessee; the Delta of Mississippi; Jackson, Mississippi; Montgomery, Alabama; Albany, Georgia; Birmingham, Alabama; Nashville, Tennessee. Each of the original sites contained a stirring moment of the Civil Rights Movement—famous march routes which we walked, a museum with artifacts like the bombed bus of the Freedom Riders, or the actual house where Martin Luther King, Jr., lived, perfectly preserved, from his books to the ashtrays and kitchen appliances. Most amazing were the speakers—for example Charles McLaurin, who'd been imprisoned in a small Mississippi jail for violating segregation laws, taking us through the cotton fields and court houses where he'd registered voters and introducing us to black mayors and sheriffs of the contemporary era.

After Memphis, Mississippi, and Alabama, the students were a bit burned out. The day's schedule usually began with us on the bus at 8:30am and continued until dinner time, with the occasional evening speaker or event. Many of them stayed up late into the night, either reading and working on their journals and reports or socializing and watching television in their hotel rooms.

I thought that South Carolina would be a great break from this hectic schedule. We had a very long bus ride to reach the Sea Islands, and many of them slept. Some of them worked on their journals while riding on the bus because, unlike me, they did not get motion sickness. When we arrived, however, most of the students were unhappy. The rustic Penn Center retreat campus, a former historically Black school with a small museum and lots of woods and fields, did not charm them. There were no televisions, no internet connection, no swimming pool, and no ice machines. The showers and bathrooms were old. After the evening program, I thought it would be nice to sit together on the old porch in rocking chairs and talk, but without their usual distractions, tensions between roommates boiled over and the hard feelings of a few spilled over onto the others. While the most adventurous of the students, who had had experience traveling in Europe, appreciated the Penn Center, everyone else seemed glad to leave for Hunting Island the next morning.

Everyone except the bus driver. As it turned out, Hunting Island park was easy for a car to navigate, but the narrow, twisting roads and the low hanging branches of the live oak trees were truly daunting for a full size bus. The driver said he would never go through this again! The experience of the ocean at this undeveloped beach was beautiful. Most of my midwestern students had never seen the Atlantic, and a few could not swim. The non-swimmers sat in the wet sand and let the soft foam of the waves surge around their legs. Having spent my childhood playing in the surf at my parents' beachfront motel in Florida, I explained sharing the ocean as a supreme act of joy, a high point of the trip, but I knew I could not ask the bus company to drive us there again.

In their evaluations, the students rated St. Helena Island the lowest of the places they visited. They couldn't see a direct connection with Civil Rights, because it was not the site of a great speech or march in which protesters were violently attacked. The speakers I had invited to their dinner program on St. Helena were a black and white teacher who worked together in the school system in the 1970s, after the civil rights movement succeeded. They quietly worked every day to provide opportunities for a diverse student body. I grieved that their work was not appreciated by my students, but I realized that the journey to St. Helena had not been worth the additional miles and days it added to the trip.

By the time my first version of the two weeks of Freedom Summer was over, the students and I were exhausted. I was literally ill with motion sickness, and I wondered if I could ever do this again. Yet many of the journals of the trip were awe-inspiring, and some said their lives had been changed. A diverse group of twenty white, African-American, and Latino women and men had made it through two weeks of intense museum-going, walking at least a mile a day on march routes, countless meals of cafeteria-style soul food, and emotionally wrenching stories of hateful speech and violence directed at non-violent demonstrators. They had a new-found respect for the bravery and "cool" of non-violent activists and their continued devotion to the principles of human rights with which they had begun.

Since that first trip by myself, I have dared to lead two more Freedom Summer classes but have pared the trip back each time to make it more sustainable, both for myself and for the mental health of the students. I took away the St. Helena trip and added nothing. Then I took out another location. I added down time on most evenings for them to explore a little on their own, or just rest and sleep. I have felt better physically on these later trips and have, therefore, been more able to be there to listen, laugh, and problem-solve with students.

In my latest evaluations, I noted that students enjoyed all the sites but complained about being too rushed in cities where the civil rights memorials have been multiplying and the museums expanding. Some of the more thoughtful and sensitive also noted that, after a while, the speakers' stories sounded similar, and they had no more emotional energy to take them in toward the end of the two weeks.

In the years since then, despite knowing that less is more, I have still felt internal pressure to show yet another documentary or add new elements to the trip. What I found in listening to the students and my co-leader, Darryl Heller, is that it is okay to turn the DVD player off and give students a chance to nap, chat, listen to music, and write in their journals. Space in between stops gives them a chance to absorb the real treasures that Les Lamon handed to me and them when he passed on the blueprint for this journey.

CHAPTER EIGHT

Ready for Class Today?

Anne Brown

I have no doubt that, as professors, we could come up with many examples of "worst matches of professor and student" in an academic setting. Here is mine. In one corner, we have the mathematics professor who values content more than pedagogy, speaks in formal language, expects perfection, and punishes errors mercilessly. In the opposite corner, we have the math-phobic elementary education major who uses a calculator for simple arithmetic, wants to teach elementary school because she "loves kids," and believes that she already knows all she needs to know about mathematics.

Grossly unfair caricatures? Yes, but there is a grain of truth here. Future elementary teachers meet mathematics professors in the math content courses required for teacher preparation at most universities, and often the results are not pretty. In the IU system, these courses are called the T-courses. I teach Math-T101, a course in which future elementary teachers explore the foundations of K-8 arithmetic, the mathematics they will someday teach.

Scores of research studies have uncovered what future and current elementary teachers do not know about the procedures and concepts of arithmetic. I have written a few of them myself. The more compelling and difficult problem is to figure out what to do about it.

About 20 years ago, I took on the task of redesigning and teaching the T-courses. The main goal of the T-courses is to teach future elementary teachers how to explain the concepts and procedures of elementary school mathematics. In the process, they should correct and refine their own knowledge, develop fluency in the written and spoken language of elementary mathematics, and become independent learners of elementary mathematics. Following an initial period in which I developed ways to meet those goals with the elementary education majors at Indiana University South Bend, there were several years in which my teaching of the courses went smoothly and my interactions with students were productive and rewarding. What worked was emphasizing how children think about mathematics and how teachers might interpret their work and help them learn. Students enjoyed the courses and found them worthwhile. I know this because they said so — in class, on the end-of-semester course evaluations, and even long after the class had ended.

A few years ago, things began to sour. Lessons, anecdotes, and classroom vignettes that had been well-received earlier were now the subject of criticism from a vocal handful of students on my evaluations. They complained that the course was too difficult and irrelevant to their futures. Some students described me as uncaring, unfair, unclear, unsympathetic to their concerns, and so forth. Some of them even spoke out in class in rude and disrespectful ways, which damaged the atmosphere for learning in the class. The complainers were a distinct minority, but, as human nature dictates, we pay a lot more attention to the negative comments of the few than the positive ones of the majority.

Not being able to discover exactly what was wrong or how to fix it, I decided to step away from teaching the T-courses. Fortunately, we have several dedicated lecturers and associate faculty in our department who were eager to teach the courses. When I stopped teaching the T-courses, I was not sure I would ever come back to them. Part of the problem was that my patience for, and creativity in, dealing with the challenges of teaching future elementary teachers were exhausted. Without fresh ideas and a new direction, it didn't make sense to try again.

A few years went by in which I mainly taught future high school teachers, math majors, and other science majors. But as coordinator of the T-courses, I kept up with what was going on. I observed the other teachers and discussed the content and pedagogy of the courses with a variety of people interested in the preparation of math teachers.

Pondering the student criticism, I realized that I had become the caricature of the math professor to these students. Their lack of interest in the subject matter also suggested that I was not doing as good a job as I had earlier in dealing with their mistaken views that they didn't need to know much about mathematics in order to teach it in elementary school. That would explain their complaints about relevance. Clearly, that had to change.

In my experience, the key to teaching any math course well is to find a way to break down the barriers between professor and students so that they will feel comfortable expressing their thoughts, especially when they are wrong. One way to do this is to offer "turn-to-your-neighbor" activities during class and circulate in the classroom, talking with individual students, and I often do that in the T-courses. However, this is an unproductive waste of time if students are not keeping up and come to class unprepared. Mathematics, as a subject, tends to be hierarchical — each new idea builds directly on prior knowledge. What students are asked to do now will often make no sense if they missed an earlier lesson. What makes this worse in the case of T101 is that math-phobic students are particularly intolerant of confusion; it paralyzes them. So, for the unprepared student, turn-to-your-neighbor activities are not just a waste of class time, they also increase the student's inertia and math-phobia. Such students simply sit there silent or complain that they have no idea what to do. When students are stuck, it takes delicate action on the part of the teacher to nudge them in the right direction without taking away the intended challenge. But a delicate action usually will not work if the student has not grasped the prerequisite concepts covered earlier in the course.

The critical question evidently boiled down to this: how do I solve the problem of students being unprepared for class? I am aware of the "just-in-time" teaching model, but the difficulty in applying it here is that I could not expect these students to read a rather formal mathematics textbook prior to class. The central and most difficult tasks for students in the course are those in which they grapple with conceptual questions, and experience has shown me that instructor input is absolutely essential for most topics.

My solution to the problem of unprepared students had its roots in several discussions I had with a colleague, Catherine Pace, who was a departmental pioneer in teaching online math courses. We talked about the benefits and challenges of teaching online courses and worked together occasionally to figure out how the available technology could be adapted to work with math courses. Initially, I was thinking only about teaching an online math course. Subsequently, this interest evolved into a project that would also transform my teaching of the face-to-face T101 course.

When the opportunity arose in the summer of 2011 to develop an online T101 course, I was ready to try it. Teaching the course online would serve students who wanted to get started with the elementary education program but could not easily get to campus to take the prerequisite T-courses. I enjoy using technology in teaching mathematics, and I was looking forward to the challenge of making it work for this class. I was hoping that stretching in this way would renew my enthusiasm for the course.

Truthfully, I also had an ulterior motive. I knew that when I worked with individual students in T101, I could still have a positive effect. I was mainly feeling uneasy in the classroom, working with large groups of T101 students whose diverse needs seemed impossible to meet simultaneously. The classroom felt like a risky place for the first time in my teaching career. Teaching an online course was a chance to reflect on and reform my teaching. The asynchronous nature of the online interactions would give me time to consider carefully what I should and should not say to motivate my students and not discourage them.

My intent in the online course was to tailor instruction and interaction to the individual. I built in many opportunities for personal interaction in the assignments that I designed and posted in Oncourse (then our learning management system). They were a mix of automatically graded short answer problems and problems requiring explanations that would be graded manually by me with written feedback. The students often had the opportunity to revise the submission based on my individualized feedback to them.

I chose to teach T101 face-to-face while I was in the process of developing the online course so I could capture my lectures and the ideas that came up in class. Honestly, I was dreading the experience. I was expecting to see the familiar lack of preparation, motivation, and engagement, as well as continued criticism from some of my students. To my surprise, this offering of T101 drew an unusually good-natured group of students who kept the classroom atmosphere upbeat and lively with their questions and humor. They asked and answered questions, argued, made jokes, helped each other, and wore costumes to class at Halloween. It wasn't the highest achieving class I ever had, but the experience working with them gave me some confidence that I could get my teaching of the course back on track. It could still be a fun course to teach.

The next semester, I taught T101 online instead of face-to-face for the first time. It was a struggle for many of the students, particularly those who were unrealistic about their time management skills and ability to use basic technology. Too many of them were not proactive in contacting me when they were having difficulty, despite frequent invitations. It was not a wholly successful experiment, but it provided me with a tested new arrangement of the course content, captured in brief, written and illustrated lectures in Oncourse. I also recorded numerous short videos to integrate with the lectures. And, more importantly, I now had a better understanding of how to support the learning of current T101 students and which course management and software tools have the potential to be effective. I also trimmed the course content to the essential ideas that I felt were needed to bring the students to the procedural and conceptual understanding of mathematics they require to be ready to teach.

The experiment with trimming the content, going for more depth rather than breadth, was partly inspired by the fairly radical approach taken to the course by a colleague (Amanda Serenevy) who has a lot of experience in the local schools with current elementary and middle-school math teachers. Her views on what content T101 students need to emphasize—fractions, fractions, and more fractions—motivated me to rethink my previous approach to the course and to get more pragmatic in what I emphasized. There is so much content that elementary education majors must learn with so much more depth than their previous mathematics education provided.

I had to make more judicious choices of which content was most critical to their future success as teachers.

Trimming the content is also necessary because it is almost impossible to cover as much content in an online course as in a face-to-face course. That may or may not be a problem. I contend that there is a yet unmeasured aspect of the online course: what do students gain from being self-directed learners who experience the content through text, video, and independent problem-solving? How can that aspect of their growth be measured? How should we compare their overall performance to that of the students in a face-to-face class?

After a summer of revision, I was ready to teach two sections of T101 in Fall 2012—one online and one face-to-face. The "aha" moment I had as I revised the materials that summer was that the course materials I had developed for use in the online course could also be used in the face-to-face course. I could now solve the preparation problem by assigning the students to study the brief, well-focused lectures before class. To make sure that they prepared, and to make sure that the online students actually read and listen to the lectures, I wrote new short, automatically graded assessments for most of the lectures (in Oncourse Tests and Surveys.) The online students completed them as part of the assigned homework, and the answers were posted. Generally, the face-to-face students completed them before class, and then we discussed the questions in class before turning to activities. I had tried this sort of "just-in-time" or "flipped" teaching in a limited way in other courses in the past, but this time, it actually seemed to be working.

Often in planning for flipped classrooms, instructors who are accustomed to lecturing for most of the period wonder what they should do with class time now. That was never an issue for me in the T-courses. I knew what I wanted to happen in class: students should work in assigned groups on problem-solving activities, and I could observe, ask questions, or intervene as needed. Now that I had an effective mechanism by which I could compel students to prepare for class, I saw the pieces falling into place. In the Fall 2012 face-to-face section, the groups worked productively on the tasks I set, diligently completed many online assignments, and generally showed impressive progress in their conceptual understanding. I was pleased with their progress.

Developing the online class thus had an unintended effect. I had almost given up hope that I would be enthusiastic about teaching this course face-to-face ever again. Having to change my teaching approach shook up my ideas about the content and delivery of the course, unlocking my creativity. I was able to capture my best ideas about teaching the mathematical content in the prepared online lectures. Now I am able to build on that material to design and carry out classroom activities to meet the course goals for the face-to-face class.

The other welcome change is that it showed me how to cut down paper-and-pencil exams to just a midterm and a final, since student knowledge could be assessed two or three times per week in the online assignments and in the face-to-face activities. I have never felt that frequent in-class exams served learning in this particular course. They were very good for finding out what the students did *not* know but not very effective in showing what they *did* know.

By the Fall of 2013, I felt that the face-to-face course was in a better place, although there is always room for improvement. The success with the Fall 2012 group proved difficult to replicate in later semesters, as the collaborative groups did not always work as productively as they did that semester. But that is a problem I have solved with other classes, and I still have ideas for improving in that area.

The online class was going much more smoothly at that point, as I now communicate stronger advice to students who are considering enrolling so they know what they are in for, and the students themselves are doing a better job with self-selecting in or out of the course. Now I am focusing mainly on improving the online course, because we have new faculty members who have taken the responsibility for teaching the face-to-face class.

Two more key changes took place in the past year that helped move the online course forward in a significant way. First, I found an excellent new textbook to use for the course that is consistent with my belief that future elementary teachers must start by reasoning about the mathematical thinking of children. Not only is the text written in a way that is very accessible to students working independently, the author has provided many examples of how to write explanations that are suitable for preparing to teach math to elementary students. My students thus have many more models to study than I can readily provide myself. This relieves me of the necessity of creating extensive written text materials and illustrations as I had in the previous version of the course. Instead, I focus on scheduling and structuring the existing materials for independent study and providing many new brief videos to further explain the most difficult aspects of the text materials. I now have much more time available to spend on individual feedback to students.

The other key improvement was switching the course management system from Oncourse to Canvas. There are many enhancements in Canvas that make the online course easier to teach, but the most important one for my courses is SpeedGrader, which allows efficient online commenting on student work using text, drawing, and high-lighting tools. The students either scan their handwritten work (the same kind of work they would produce in a face-to-face class) or use a word processing and drawing program to provide the technical detail that mathematics homework requires. This allows me to simply assign problems from the textbook that require them to "provide an explanation in numbers, pictures and words," instead of creating my own objective questions to test the conceptual material, which is a difficult and time-consuming task. Grading their electronic work is much quicker, and it is easier for me to point out exactly what parts of their work need to be improved. Students were generally pleased with the course in Fall 2014, giving a rating of excellent in most of the categories on the course evaluations. I can still see aspects of the course that can be improved, but it is getting much closer to a course of the same richness as the face-to-face version.

To sum up, teaching T101 online has resulted in a cycle of creativity that I am enjoying immensely. Stepping away from a course for a few semesters and then trying a new pedagogy can be a great way to refresh your creativity and boost your energy for making the innovations needed to meet the challenges in any course you teach. Reflecting on my teaching experiences over the years reminds me of what I have learned again and again: making major changes in your teaching always solves some problems and opens up new avenues for progress, but it also creates new problems to solve. And, as Will Rogers said, "Even if you are on the right track, you'll get run over if you just sit there!"

CHAPTER NINE

A Teacher's To-Do List

Rebecca Brittenham

I walk through the classroom, a training workshop I am about to run for fledgling college teachers. I can see that most of the participants are here, dispersed around tables, with no one venturing toward the front of the room. Most are graduate students with freshly minted MA degrees, some I know to be highly competent students and superb writers from my own graduate classes, but only a few have prior teaching experience or training. There are ripples of anxiety in the room, edging through the conversations and erupting in nervous laughter. As I move among them, handing out packets, exchanging greetings, I can hear how worried they are about all the details of the upcoming semester: "How many weeks should I allow for each paper? How many points should I deduct for absences and missing work? How will I know if I've prepared enough material to fill a seventy-five minute class? What will I do if the students don't *talk*?" Their anxiety is contagious, and I can feel its clutch in my stomach: they're not ready; I can't possibly get them ready in time; how can I hope to convey everything they need to know?

"The classroom is malleable," I am telling the teacher trainees later that day, moving them around and demonstrating as we go.

"You can work with your students to reshape the space, keep them from stiffening up, cluster them this way or that way to make them feel safer, send them up to the board in groups, in pairs, let them take charge of the computer up front or the chalkboard, move your own body out of or into the limelight like this, try moving away from the student who is speaking like this, so she will project toward her peers. Try being the slowest person in the room to find the passage everyone is analyzing; let them show you where to find it; let them explain what it means." They are warming up, practicing on one another, making plans, but I'm still inwardly anxious: in my efforts to provide them with a range of strategies, with a structure they can lean on, I'm failing to convey my real sense that teaching is an endless process of rethinking and reconstruction, a constant risky act of becoming rather than a comfortably settled roster of best practices. I'm worried that in the pressure to take on this new role as the classroom authority they will feel stuck channeling a teacher they once had, hemmed in by the mystical paradigms of "good" and "bad" teaching that pervade our psyches. I want them to know that it's okay for a while to feel like a fraud, but I also need to convey on some level that becoming a good teacher is about getting past the fraudulence to find a kind of truth between yourself and your students.

In hindsight, I wish I had preempted the agenda for that day and asked them all to make lists: lists of everything they were worried about and everything they were excited about; lists of all the questions they needed covered by the workshop; lists of qualities and techniques used by their favorite and least favorite teachers; lists of activities they could stage in the classroom; lists of possible uses for each piece of classroom equipment.

Things You Can Do with a Podium Mounted on a Table at the Front of a Classroom

1. Standing well behind it, place a sheaf of notes on it, and hold forth for seventy-five minutes, being careful to roll your eyes toward the ceiling in order to ignore all the texting going on in the front row.

2. Set it on the floor under the table very gently so as not to make too much of a clunk, come out from behind the table, and find out who your students are.

3. Ceremoniously place it in the middle of the classroom and invite students to try balancing on it with one leg, as a device to center themselves and retain needed oxygen for an 8:30 a.m. class.

Weeks into the semester, when my student teachers are busy teaching their students, I am registering once again how hard it is to convey anything about the reality of teaching without getting sucked into false sentiments and pre-scripted narrative arcs. I keep returning to the reality of my own teaching lists, which represent more than anything the dog paddle methods I actually use to get through a semester.

Things to Do on Tuesday
- Finish W130 drafts and hand back
- Photocopy sample student paragraph for W130
- Prep Ehrenreich for W130
- Grade W350 Quiz
- Start grading W350 papers
- Read Personnel Files
- Letter for M___ by Friday
- Email J____ re: Leadership Academy
- Post Assess on Website

- Read B___ 's thesis proposal
- Call adoption committee meeting
- Decide on book order!
- Draft FRG
- Smart Research Award: 2 pg. summary, Faculty letter, $250
- Fish
- Waffles
- Ginger
- 5 Lemons
- Garbanzo Beans

One of the great satisfactions of a "To Do List" is to look back and cross off things one has accomplished. Knowing this, I've begun to add mundane items to all the mental and physical lists I make that I imagine will later provide self-congratulatory fodder. So far I have held back on items like "stand up and stretch right after this" or "put all books and papers in a bag for morning" or "get to the bathroom," things I know I will likely be doing anyway and are thus not cause for undue celebration (though getting to pee in between classes and meetings is frequently a tricky personal luxury and should be duly appreciated). Also intertwined in these lists are essential though unwritten messages: "breathe," "hydrate," "stand up straight," "go home to your family."

Sometimes I have so many lists going that I start losing them or losing track of the intention behind them, so this semester I'm keeping a notebook dedicated to holding all my "To Do" lists together. Suddenly there seems to be a hierarchy of lists: lists that deserve to be in the book and undeserving lists.

Lists That Deserve to Be in the Notebook

- Lists of things to grade (a procrastination technique since I remember them perfectly well)
- Sublists of student names whose papers I have responded to or haven't responded to or have read but have no idea how to respond to (another procrastination technique)
- Lists of students I need to track down for conferences
- Lists of students scheduled for conferences
- Lists of students who were scheduled for conferences but did not show up
- Lists of students scheduled for advising
- Book orders (due Oct. 5, now overdue!)
- List of students to recommend for peer mentoring
- List of teacher training workshops for the spring
- List of classes with no teachers for the spring
- List of books people tell me to read
- List of research projects I must accomplish this year or consider myself an abject failure.

Grocery lists, menus for dinner parties, and lists of things I could plant in the garden next spring do not deserve to go in the notebook but inevitably slip in. This list is in the notebook, but I don't remember what it means:

- "Revising, replaying, inverting"
- "Trans-contextualizing"
- Check Barthes *S/Z*
- Complicity and distance?
- Bert is evil Website

Eventually it occurs to me that these were notes for a conference paper on parody delivered at the Midwest Modern Language Association last spring. Reminder to revise that paper into an article while material still clear in head shows up on another To-Do list (cf. abject failure item above), which does belong in the notebook but is not there.

Lists That Don't Need to Be in the Notebook

The names and faces and major writing obstacles of every single student in my W130 class; they slide through my closed eyelids like rosary beads. One student smiled in class for the first time yesterday—he lit up, incandescent. We were working on commas; who knew that coordinate conjunctions were the thing that could finally reach him. Another student was so excited about her paper in our last conference: "I'm getting it, Mrs. Brittingham, I'm really getting it this time!" Why hasn't she been back to class since then?

I'm starting to hate the notebook of lists, possibly because I made the mistake of labeling it *The To-Do Book of Lists*, which seems to give the lists in there a terrifying solidity. I frequently leave the notebook behind at the office or at home and find myself reverting back to scraps of paper, the flip sides of envelopes offering to update my subscription to *Atlantic Monthly* and *AARP Magazine*, and post-its of various sizes that cling to the insides of handbags, attach themselves to my Fresca can, lose themselves among stacks of student papers, or end up holding my place in books.

List Attached to Fresca Can

- Check Attendance—notify students if failing
- WriteWell reminders to struggling students
- Milk

- Eng Muff
- Manchego
- Olives
- Mortadella

This was an actual post-it that went AWOL when needed at the grocery store and turned up as a bookmark in a book that a colleague loaned me to read as background for a graduate student poetry thesis. The list itself proved unnecessary since the grocery store items were self-evident, and I had been obsessing about the failing and struggling students for weeks.

In W130 today we are working on Mike Rose's amazing analysis of all the hand/brain operations involved in doing good work, whether it's waitressing or neurosurgery. The piece we're reading is based on interviews Rose did with his mother, Maria; she sounds like some of the waitresses at Nick's Patio, the twenty-four-hour Greek diner in South Bend, who treat with equal precision and kindness the old folks eating creamed beef at four o'clock in the afternoon, the kids grinding Greek chicken and rice particles into the vinyl seat covers, and the drunk twenty-somethings eating scrambled eggs, sausage, and French toast at four o'clock in the morning. My students are assembled in practice four-tops trying to recite one another's break-fast orders from memory and analyzing the hand/brain operations described in the reading. I overhear R____ saying, "This is totally the opposite of Barbara Ehrenreich. I think the real point is human dignity" and yell from across the room, "Write that down!" Students look bewildered, and I realize they're not sure who I'm talking to.

Hand/Brain Operations Involved in Teaching

1. Planning how to prompt a discussion on Ehrenreich while running down three flights of stairs at 8:28am with fifteen graded papers, three books, two post-it notes covered with notes, a pen, a dry erase marker, and a cup of tea.

2. Setting up group work while noticing who hasn't made a single note on the reading and who doesn't even have the book, while becoming peripherally aware that a student who has been missing for three weeks has suddenly appeared in the doorway making mysterious summoning motions.

3. Synthesizing a class discussion of a sample paragraph while taking notes for revision on the displayed computer screen, trying to remember how to spell Ehrenreich, and planning a follow-up exercise on thesis development based on the same sample paragraph. (Students helpfully supply spelling of Ehrenreich and remind me to post the revised paragraph and sample thesis on our course website — they are always encouraging.)

4. Handing back graded papers with one hand, clutching a stream of incoming homework with the other, and overhearing two students speculate on whether they can leave now while responding to another student who is explaining the medical condition that prevented him from finishing the paper and that he needs a copy of the assignment because he can't access it online, when another student reports from the back of the lab that the printer has jammed.

Yesterday I assigned the footnotes from David Foster Wallace's essay, "Tense Present," in my English W350 class. Found myself howling with laughter while prepping the essay — had to stuff my coat under the office door so colleagues would not think me insane. Students seemed singularly unimpressed with the essay, but they worked assiduously in groups identifying the functions of the footnote convention, then began reporting back that Wallace is elitist, pretentious, way too happy with himself. Restrained myself from pleading, "but did you get to the part about all the wedgies he was given as a child?" "What about the line where our 'hairy ancestors were sitting around in the veldt' developing language norms like 'Knock these two rocks together and you can start a fire.' That's hilarious, right?" Instead found myself mentioning casually, "Well, maybe not that happy with himself, since he killed himself at forty-six." Nineteen pairs of eyes swivel. "Yup," I say, "His wife came home and found he'd hanged himself on the patio." Suddenly everyone is interested in Wallace; they are busy drawing parallels with Virginia Woolf, whom we read a month ago, and finding inner turmoil revealed in the play of footnotes against the body of the text. Is playing the suicide card a cheap trick? Realize gradually that my students have a good case against Wallace as elitist and suggest ways to integrate a critique into their upcoming papers.

Ways to Commit Suicide and Possibly Thereby Achieve Literary Fame
- Wrist-slitting
- Hanging
- Walking into a river with rock-laden pockets
- Defenestration
- Jumping off bridge
- Throwing self under a pastry truck
- Sleeping pill overdose, gas oven, or car exhaust
- Most hackneyed: bullet in brain
- Less common: seppuku

On a constraining scrap scavenged from the breakfast table newspaper, I make a list of four different exercises I want to set up in my W350 class, with the various prompts I intend to use. Take the scrap into class and promptly spill tea on it. Since the class is about the conventions of the list form, I can only laugh and display the tea-blurred artifact—students appear amused. They are very kind always.

Lists That Don't Need to Be Written Down

1. What I'm planning to do in class today because it's burning on my brain, and I'm constructing and reconstructing the possibilities right up to the minute, then the structure is in play and, if it's working, the students take it somewhere that wouldn't be on the list anyway.
2. What I'm making for dinner. Ditto.
3. Students who aren't showing up for class, because they are the worry beads I sort through while eating, driving in the car, and photocopying samples for class.

I know so many things about teaching these days—a hundred million things I want to tell those teachers in training. Sometimes I feel giddy just thinking about the fifty thousand ways you can orchestrate learning in a classroom so that even the sterile walls and computer screen, the desk and table arrangements, the lights and window fittings seem to become the malleable prop for a theater of the divine that features the intellectual willingness of twenty-one people to bring the best of themselves to the room and share it with others. So why is it that I'm still so green at this?

References

Wallace, D. (2001). Tense Present: Democracy, Usage, and the Wars over English. *Harper's Magazine*, (302.1811).

CHAPTER TEN

Teaching Art My Way

Tuck Langland

I majored in Art because I liked it, and after receiving the BA, I considered earning a living, which ideally would be by teaching sculpture on the college level. So I entered the Master of Fine Arts program in Sculpture at the University of Minnesota, the MFA being the essential terminal degree for a professorship in studio art. But on reflection, I found it quite interesting that, though the degree was leading me to be a teacher, there were no courses in *how* to teach. All the course work was on how to make art, plus some art history.

Approaching graduation for my treasured MFA, I began looking for a job and found that they were scarce — about two or three a year in this country — and were being taken by candidates with extensive and glamorous resumes, of which I had neither. So my wife and I took a daring leap, booked on a ship to England, and arrived in that foreign country in the middle of the summer of 1964 to look for a college spot. It was, in retrospect, insanity.

But it would only be insanity if it didn't work, and it did. I found a job up in Carlisle, right near the Scottish border. We moved there and found an inexpensive small house about 50 feet from the site of Hadrian's Wall and a short walk to the Carlisle College of Art. On the first day of classes, I walked there and was met by a somewhat older man who asked, "Who are you?" I answered, "I'm the sculpture teacher." He got an odd look on his face, then said, "But *I AM* the sculpture teacher." After that awkward moment he learned that while he was on summer holiday, they had hired me as a second teacher to assist him for the year. His name was Dennis Westwood, and we are great friends to this day. I see him often and speak with him on the phone regularly.

Then began my first real introduction to teaching sculpture, not as any kind of academic subject, but as true hands-on work. The first class I had was a group of about 15 high school students on an advanced pre-college course. We set up modeling stands in a big circle, each student got a wire armature for a figure, and we placed a model in the center of the circle. She was named Olga, and local lore had it that she had a history as a stripper somewhere. She dropped her robe with a flourish, gave a shake and a ta-da, bum-de-bum wiggle, then let all her swinging endowments settle down and looked right at the students. I saw they were virtually paralyzed. One student was so traumatized he turned his back on her entirely and made a sort of lumpy vaguely human form, whose head was a disk on which he stuck some vague features, like Mr. Potato Head. How was I to deal with this?

Well, as they say, "chuck 'em in the deep end to learn to swim." I began paddling.

We had a great year eventually, Dennis and I, and with him helping and encouraging, we nurtured those first-time students into getting over their fears and actually looking at — examining closely — the naked woman before them. They turned in some pieces, which if not masterworks, were a far cry from their beginnings.

At the end of that first year, the job in Carlisle was over, so I did some interviews and we moved to Sheffield, where the job was better. This time I was team-teaching with three other sculptors, and that's when my real education as a teacher of studio art took off. By working with the team, listening to what the others were saying in class, participating in long gab sessions in the office, plus going it alone on occasion, I began to figure out some important things about teaching a course so dependent on the individual.

I'll return to that in a moment, but after three years in England, we had a child and decided to head home, so I found a job in Murray, Kentucky, and we moved there. Talk about a culture shock! But it was also a teaching shock, since I now had a large building for sculpture, with quite a bit of good equipment, and the classes were all my own. By this time I had learned a lot. Isn't it true that you only really begin to learn when you begin to teach?

And after four years in Murray, in 1971, I found a job in South Bend, and we moved there, now with two children. Again, I was the solo sculpture teacher. I was given two run-down houses to try to teach in, which were about impossible, and the next year a larger house, and four years after that I convinced the administration to rent an off-campus industrial building for me.

But now it was a different ball game. I had a building, and I was able to make it my own, buy the equipment we needed, install a bronze foundry, and run the classes my way, which was as though the students were apprentices to a professional artist. It was all off campus, so I didn't hang around the proverbial water cooler with other professors, and no one ever seemed to come to see what or how I was doing. I was quite isolated.

Not long ago, I listened to a Lundquist lecture in which the Fellow talked about constantly testing his students on a wide variety of topics related to the course. There would be at least a test a week, often more, usually of the multiple guess variety. At the question period I raised my hand and asked, "What would you suggest for a class in which there are no wrong answers?"

That is what a studio art class is. There is no hard and fast, right or wrong material to learn. There is, rather, an avenue, a means for the student to do something — something personal, something no one else in the world can do just the same. My job as teacher, then, is to make that happen. And there are two parts to that. One is to provide the technical means and skills to make what they envision in their heads. The other part is to convince them that there are no wrong answers, that nothing happens right the first time, and to overcome their innate fear of failure. That is the psychologist part.

For a couple of years, we had a student in the sculpture classes who was retired after a career as the advertising guy at Robertson's department store. He was perhaps seventy at the time. But he created more daring, more experimental, more exciting work than the young students, and the reason was, at seventy, he had nothing at all to lose. I used to hold him up as an example of how the young ones, too, could loosen up, drop the fear of failure that had been hammered into them from kindergarten on, and be a bit more free and daring. He was among my best teaching assistants.

My international experiences weren't over. In 1977, I managed a teacher exchange with Dennis. My wife and I went to Stoke-on-Trent in England with our two daughters, and he came to South Bend with his wife and son. We swapped houses, studios, jobs, and cars for a year. Again I was thrown into a team-teaching situation, except that the rest of the team did little teaching. After my solo teaching job, I found it easy to carry my end.

Yet another foreign experience came in 1992 when the U.S. Information Agency invited me to Kampala, Uganda, to teach bronze casting at Makerere University, in cooperation with Francis Nnag-genda, the foremost sculptor in East Africa, whom I had brought to our campus in 1975.

Now here was another shock to which I had to adapt. When I visited the sculpture studios, I found there were no running water and no power tools except for a bench grinder, and the wires were stripped bare and just shoved in the socket — and it was 220 volts! So I went into town and bought a plug, but when I got back, I realized I should have bought a screwdriver as well. The place had next to nothing, and I was supposed to cast bronze.

Again, chucked into the deep end.

The students looked at me with skepticism, so I found materials to model a portrait head, hired a model, and knocked one off pretty quickly. That was my credential. It worked, and the students' attitude changed completely. By this time I was confident enough that I could manage just about anything, and with the now eager students helping, within a week we were casting our first bronzes, melting the metal (well, it wasn't really bronze, just scrap yellow stuff) in an old English furnace, using not gas but oil for fuel — not fuel oil either, but oil drained from the crankcase of a truck after 30,000 miles, whether it needed it or not.

We made little sculptures out of wax, and soon people were showing up out of the woodwork wanting to make pieces, and my attitude was "Y'all come. Let's have fun together while we learn." If I had to have a philosophy of teaching, that would be it.

Again, there were no wrong answers, no academic rigor, but an enthusiastic crowd of folks experiencing something they had never experienced before, and taking home with them nice little bronze birds and animals and heads and figures and even some abstractions. We cast about fifty works in my six weeks there. And because there were no wrong answers, the creativity exploded, and some very wonderful works emerged, works which I felt could never have happened if there were grades and such looming over them.

Back at Indiana University South Bend, I was also teaching Art Appreciation, a lecture course, in the small auditorium to about eighty-five students at a time. Nearly all of them were taking it as a requirement. Many confessed they weren't at all interested in art, but had to sit there. Also, one semester, an older retired couple I knew wanted to audit the course, and they were told it cost full tuition, which they gladly paid. So I thought, they are paying good money just to listen to me. I'd better be good.

It was a slide lecture format, with no small break-out groups or anything like that. I tried to select slides which would illustrate the vast array of exciting world art and arrange them chronologically, so they were subliminally learning history at the same time. I worked on things like moving around the stage so my voice would come from different places, using a strong voice, thinking I was speaking to someone in the back row, and changing slides often enough so they didn't get bored with looking at the same one. And, of course, I would use humor to keep things light and keep up interest. I even had a streaker once. That livened things up!

The student reviews were all positive, with a large number saying they had planned on hating the course, but it turned out to be their favorite.

I still like to lecture now, fourteen years retired, because the lessons I learned about the relationship between a college lecture and show-biz are still with me. And I am serious about the show-biz part. I have noticed that when a person is reading a speech, boredom sets in, but when they stray from the printed page and ad lib a bit, it suddenly becomes more interesting. So I vowed never to use notes.

If I didn't know the material, including dates and specifics, I would learn it, not read it. As for the overall arc of the lectures, my slides were my notes.

I suspect humans are about the only creatures on earth who regularly assemble in large numbers, all facing the same way, while one person stands before them and does all the talking. It's part of our nature, I guess. Many teaching situations can break that norm with circles of chairs, round table discussions, etc., but with 85 students and no provisions for break-out sessions, that wasn't going to happen. So I had to make it fun and exciting and put in as much solid information as I could.

So, in the end, my teaching career has differed from most in that the "sculpture part" was part art, part sculpture techniques, part psychology, part counseling, part being a mechanic keeping the machines running, part janitor. The "lecturing part" was part show-biz, part art history professor, and part designer/implementer of tests to really dig out what they had learned. I never used multiple choice or true/false but made them come up with answers on their own. I also had them write what I called "essayettes," short three or four sentence answers to specific questions, only answers they did not select but dredged up from their learning.

So, here comes the most important part. In order to be a good teacher, I think a professor must be engaged in his or her field. For me, that meant maintaining a large and well-equipped studio on my property, making my own sculpture every free moment, entering shows to compete with other artists, and seeking out large commissions, often in competition with others who were full-time sculptors. In other words, I was in the game, the real game. I was constantly refining and revising such things as formulas for the bronze molds, kinds of rubber to use for molds, types of clay to work with, and so on. I also visited major sculptors all over the US and Europe, became a member of the National Sculpture Society so I could hang out with the top figure sculptors in the nation, visited every museum and gallery I could, and read widely on the subject.

When IU was interviewing for a new Chancellor (the time Una Mae Reck was selected in early 2000), one faculty member asked each of the candidates this question: "What do you think a university is?"

I've thought about that ever since, and my answer is that, among a great many things, there are three crucial elements of the institutions we call universities. First is job training. Why else would we have accounting and dental hygiene schools? The second is life enrichment. Why else study Chaucer or biology if you're going to be a special education teacher? And third is research, which contributes to the sum total of knowledge of the human race.

In my case, I wasn't going to make artists out of students in the art appreciation class, but I was going to make more savvy museum goers, since many entered the class never having been to one. In sculpture, I was teaching the top methods, what the professionals used, so that if someone did want to become a sculptor, he or she would have the tools, and if not, at least he or she would understand the field. But, in both cases, there was an enrichment process, a widening of horizons, a greater depth of understanding of the importance of art to a society. This, to me, was teaching art.

I can't say if I was a great teacher or not. I was certainly popular, but greatness is more than that. What I can say is that I did it my way, urging the students to do it their way.

CHAPTER ELEVEN

The More I Teach the Less I Know

Jay VanderVeen

I am not young enough to know everything.
— Oscar Wilde

I thought I knew it all. With a newly minted PhD diploma in hand and one whole semester of teaching as junior faculty under my belt, I had all the knowledge that was required to handle a new class. A major research university wouldn't have given me that degree if I did not have all the answers. Another college wouldn't have put the effort into hiring me if they were not certain I could handle the position. I demonstrated my skills by writing a dissertation, by winning awards as an instructor (albeit one who assisted an actual professor in a giant introductory course), and by generally being an all-around clever guy. I was fearless. I knew it all. Or so I thought.

My new course was a hit even before it started. It was about forensics, and few things are sexier than the study of dead bodies. At least this was true according to television programmers, since it seemed that half the networks' shows airing at 10pm had something to do with determining whether the victim died of blunt force trauma to the head. In reality, the field of forensic anthropology does not involve million dollar futuristic laboratories where beautiful people in white coats and edgy hairstyles solve crimes in 42 minutes. Instead, my course would explore the application of biological anthropology to the legal process of death investigation. Still, the skills I would teach were designed to prepare students for graduate study or for future work in association with forensic science specialists. At the same time, I was sure that my course would also magically transform them into better critical thinkers and bestow upon them the ability to be more scientifically literate. I knew it would. My plan was to divide the semester into two major parts: the fundamentals and the application of that knowledge. In the first unit of the class, the students worked together in groups to plan a mock recovery of an unidentified dead body. A week before the "investigation," we discussed what equipment might be needed and they decided who would bring which items. On the day of the assignment, the groups were led to their crime scenes and worked collectively to document the evidence. They delegated roles and did their best to collect and record anything that appeared important. At the end of the class period, they formulated how to disseminate their information to each group member, because, although the group worked together, each student's answers to the crime scene project had to be his or her own. This unit worked well. Students were motivated, they learned, and they demonstrated their learning on assignments.

The next section of the course focused on the anatomy of the human body. This is necessary because most forensic anthropologists spend their time determining the age, sex, and ancestry of the victim from skeletal characteristics. I explained the anatomy in a very complete manner. I gave them the Greek and Latin translations of the names for each bone and bone feature. They were provided with pictures and page numbers to which they could refer. The students correctly answered all of the questions I posed to them during class. Like me, they knew their stuff forward and back.

The morning of the big bone test, a group of students was studying together on the floor next to the classroom door. At the appointed hour, the whole class was outside waiting for me to finish setting up the various stations with the bones they needed to identify. It was stressful for them, just as it was designed to be. I had given this test before, or a close approximation of it, as a graduate instructor. I had taken this test, too, as a student myself. I knew what the students were feeling. What I didn't know was how little they knew.

No one passed the test. Not a single student correctly identified more than 60 percent of the bone features or other materials. They flat out failed. It was a monumental failure unlike any I had ever experienced before in my academic career. I quadruple-checked the answer key. It was easier to circle correct answers on the exam. My red grading pen ran out of ink. I didn't know if my expectations were too high or the students' were too low. I thought we had bonded, the students and I. They really enjoyed the first section of the class and succeeded in that assessment. They may not have had as much fun learning to identify the bones, but they never complained. Answers were volunteered in response to my questions in class. No one came to my office hours expressing trepidation. Everything seemed fine with the class to that point. Regardless, they didn't know what they should. Or maybe, just maybe, I didn't know how to teach it.

I feared going to class the next day, but I walked in with a pile of papers in my arms and sat down on the table at the front of the room. The students could tell by the look on my face that things had changed. Upon finishing the test, they had probably guessed how poorly they had done. I began a conversation with the students about how their failure was my failure. They had failed to understand the knowledge needed to continue in the course, and I had failed to grasp that. I had failed to deliver proper instruction. We talked about how the plans for the semester would need to be thrown out, because the class could not continue until this material was learned. Everything that followed built on the knowledge of how the bones are supposed to look and fit together. I would be unable to teach without using the proper terminology. We would have to begin the anatomy section all over again and get it right.

In my mind, I was already reading the students' evaluations of the course and of me. I expected the worst. I knew that I was responsible for the worst class in the history of the department, of the school, maybe even the entire university. But rather than becoming angry over their scores or frustrated with my teaching methods, the students allowed me to revise the course schedule so that we could spend additional time on the material. They knew they needed to know the skeleton.

They also needed to know that I cared, so I asked them what would help. At the students' request, I posted the slides for the day's lecture online. I noticed that many of the students printed these out to help with taking notes or annotated them online. I also created review games for the students. After three or four class lectures, I passed around Bingo boards. The students filled in terms selected from a list I provided. I then showed them slides of skeletal anatomy, and they checked off the part if it was on their game board. The winners had to prove that they had correctly identified five elements in a row. The students seemed to enjoy this style of review; many were quite competitive in their efforts to earn the small prizes I offered. As a result of our collaborative efforts and a form of "gamification," they all passed the exam the next time.

What's more, they built on the experience. For the final part of the class, I gave them the task of putting what they learned into practice. They were provided access to two sets of real human remains. All those bone names and locations they worked so hard to learn were now used in determining whether the skeletal material came from a male or female, the age the individual may have been at death, how long he or she had been dead, and what other traits we could discern that would help to provide a basis for identification. This time, however, they formed groups even though I didn't ask them to do so. They asked each other questions, accessed the resources I provided them online, cracked open the textbook, and Googled anything they did not know. Their answers varied, but most of the students approached the correct range of traits.

Again, this evaluation of their learning was made into a game of sorts, and they relished the opportunity to "level up" by completing the task. After the assignment was handed in, but before it was graded and returned, the students were asked to discuss in class what the correct age, sex, and other identifiable elements were for the skeletons. The general consensus was surprisingly accurate. They seemed to pay more attention to the answers when their colleagues provided their own thoughts than when I returned an assignment marked up in red with a score at the top. I have used these debriefings in other classes since then. I think they are effective in gauging the accuracy of my perception of what the students needed to complete assignments, to know what they know, and also as a way in which they can continue to learn from each other.

A number of students who have taken the class (which I continue to teach every few semesters) have later accompanied me to the Dominican Republic on archaeological research. While there, they have been faced with the exact same situation, only this time it is real. They have needed to identify, as best as can be done, remains housed in cardboard boxes at a local museum or, in one case, offered to me in a duffel bag. With only their training and some advice from me, they have succeeded at the tasks. This was the ultimate test, and if those students could pass it, the others likely can, too.

But what do I know?

What I do know is this: one shouldn't stop trying to learn, and one shouldn't give up after the first mistake. The students who failed the midterm ended up being some of the best students I have had the pleasure to teach, the ones I still remember. They've completed graduate school, published papers, gotten jobs in and out of the field, and they still keep in touch. They didn't take my grade as a statement on their overall ability. Nor did they hold my failings against me as a teacher. Together, we all learned more from that experience than if I had curved the exam and everyone got an average grade. In every one of my classes, I take ownership of the questions on any evaluative measure. About twice a semester, I tell students that I am throwing out one of the items on their quiz or test. It is a policy now to discard any question to which fewer than half the class answered as I intended. Needless to say, we talk about the question, sometimes at length. It is not as if I am giving up on the idea that they were supposed to know, but I am confident enough to tell them that I did something poorly and that I am going to fix the mistake. They seem to appreciate seeing faculty members acknowledge mistakes.

The students learn that we don't know it all, but as a team we can learn a little more than we did before. I make a point of opening up discussions in class on a variety of topics outside my expertise so that students can see me actively listening, responding when I can, and directing the question back to the entire class to ferret out feedback. When we are all stumped, I make a show of writing down the question in my notes. After class, I go back to my office and seek out the answer, and within the hour, I post the best answer I can find on the course website for all to read. In this way, the students are watching the process of inquiry happen right before their eyes.

So now, after fourteen years of teaching, I know less than I knew at the start. This is not what I expected to happen, but it has made me a better teacher. Yes, there is still more I need to know.

CHAPTER TWELVE

Changing My Mindset

Carolyn A. Schult

Once upon a time, long, long ago, I was a dreadful teacher. Over time, I transformed into an excelent teacher. This didn't come about through enchanted kisses or fairy godmothers, but through lots of effort, time, embarrassing failures, and sometimes painful self-reflection. The journey from dreadful to excellent was a long, hard slog for me. Like many college professors, my first teaching experience was as a teaching assistant at a large, research-focused university. The professor handled the lecture hall full of 300 students, and the graduate students met with smaller discussion sections of 25 students to provide a more enriching experience for the students. Because I had attended a small liberal arts college where all the classes were taught by full-time faculty, the entire system was foreign to me. I had no experience with teaching assistants, and I wasn't quite sure what the job entailed. So I started asking questions: How do I do this job? What do I need to know?

The professor I was assisting offered this advice, "Smile a lot, learn your students' names, and remember what side of the desk you sit on — never date your students."

I hastened to assure her that I would never think of dating a student but would get to know them and would try to be cheerful.

I tried again to get more information: "But that doesn't really answer my question. What do I actually *do* in the discussion sections?"

"Don't worry," she said. "You have to go to TA training. They'll help you."

The training for Teaching Assistants consisted of a one-credit-hour course that I was required to take during the same semester that I started teaching. The only training I received before the semester actually began was a diversity workshop to make sure I wouldn't discriminate against women or minorities in the classroom, which was valuable information, but I still didn't know what to actually *do* in the classroom when the semester started. To make matters worse, my discussion sections were scheduled early in the week, before our weekly TA meeting with the professor. The meetings were intended to allow the professor to tell us what points to emphasize and to give us advice about how to present material. The meeting would also allow us to share different approaches to the material and to voice any concerns we had. Because I taught first, then went to the TA meeting, our meetings became an embarrassing ritual of pointing out what I should have done rather than helping me plan what to do. I would hear: "What do you mean, you covered topic A instead of B? Didn't you know B was far more important?"

Needless to say, that first semester did not go well. I was dreadful, in both senses of the word. I was an awful teacher, and I was scared to go into the classroom each week. Looking back on the minimal training and lack of support I received, I can see now that the blame was not entirely mine. At the time, however, I was devastated. I was a failure at something I cared deeply about. Teaching had been a dream of mine for so long, but it seemed I just didn't have it in me to be a good teacher. I didn't know so many things — how to connect with the students, how to start discussions, how to design group projects and classroom activities, how to lecture at a level that complemented rather than repeated the reading assignments. I knew that other grad students weren't struggling the same way I had, which made me feel even worse. As part of my TA training, I observed a friend and fellow first-time teacher, Gina, who was a great teacher. She engaged the students in a wide-ranging discussion of the course material, challenging the students to think deeply about public policy, to think multiple steps into the future, and to justify their positions with evidence, not opinion. It was a wonderful class, and depressing as hell for me. Gina had a gift for teaching, a talent for engaging students and pushing them to think critically about important issues. She made it seem effortless. How could I ever match that? I didn't have her gift.

I didn't realize it at the time, but I was mired in what psychologist Carol Dweck calls a "fixed mindset" (Dweck, 2006). People with fixed mindsets see basic qualities, such as talent, personality, or intelligence, as fixed traits. You either have it or you don't. When bad things happen, it's a sign of your incompetence and lack of worth. Your failures become a part of your self-concept. According to a fixed mindset, teachers are born, not made.

In contrast, people with a "growth mindset" see those basic qualities as more malleable, able to be developed through commitment and hard work (Dweck, 2006). Failures are a sign that they need to work harder and smarter. According to a growth mindset, teachers can always learn to be better.

I didn't have the benefit of Dweck's research to guide me back then. All I knew was I had to figure out how to be a better teacher. I needed to teach to pay my way through graduate school. My liberal arts alma mater had not shown me how to be a good teaching assistant, but it had given me significant experience in problem solving, research, and collaborative learning. I might not be able to teach well, but I knew how to learn well, so why couldn't I learn how to teach? Without knowing it, I had started changing to a growth mindset.

Research shows that those with a growth mindset are far more accurate in evaluating their current abilities, even when the information is unflattering (Dweck, 2006). By looking at themselves honestly, they are able to formulate more realistic plans for growth. The first thing I did after vowing to learn how to teach was to swallow my pride and admit I needed help. I had been afraid to ask for help after my first futile questions to my supervising professor, not wanting to seem unprepared or utterly lacking in ability. At this point, I had nothing left to lose, so I freely asked for advice from my fellow graduate students and my professors. In a strange paradox, asking all those questions raised their opinion of my teaching. My friends and professors were impressed that I cared so much about my teaching. They saw my constant questions as a sign that I was working hard at it.

And I was. I spent considerable time visiting other graduate students' classes, including my friend Gina's. While the students took notes on the content of the class, I took notes on specific questions the instructors asked to start a discussion, specific examples they used to illustrate difficult concepts, and specific exercises they assigned to demonstrate how the concepts work in the real world. I was building a library of the nuts and bolts of an engaging, entertaining lecture, but I still wasn't confident about going off script and attempting the wide-ranging, free-flowing discussions that had impressed me so much from Gina's class.

Eventually, an opportunity for just such a discussion arose in my class. I was teaching about teratogens, substances such as drugs or alcohol that can cause harm to a developing fetus when ingested by a pregnant woman. I was explaining that many of these harmful effects are completely preventable, and thus we need more effective education and treatment efforts to help pregnant women abstain from drugs and alcohol. A habitually quiet student suddenly spoke up and forcefully stated that any pregnant woman who drank alcohol or used drugs should be put into jail for the duration of her pregnancy. Now this was a terrible idea for a number of reasons, but I stopped myself from saying so. I took a deep breath while I tried to sort through all the questions racing through my mind at that moment. Would the other students be able to see the flaws in this plan? Did they care enough about this topic to debate the pros and cons? The forceful student was a big guy. I mean really big — Big Ten defensive tackle big. Would any student dare contradict him? WWGD — What Would Gina Do?

"Let's explore this idea a bit," I said, in my best Gina impression, and I started asking questions. The class responded slowly, tentatively, but they responded, and with just a few pauses and stammers, I guided them through a discussion that questioned the justice of laws that only applied to pregnant women. We considered the physical realities of addiction and the strong reluctance of treatment programs to take in pregnant women. This discussion led them to see for themselves the unintended consequences of such a seemingly well-intentioned policy. Defensive Tackle had only wanted to protect the fetus. Through the discussion, the students realized that when faced with jail, drug-using pregnant women would try to avoid detection by avoiding medical care, which could have far greater harmful effects to the fetus. Defensive Tackle seemed content with the outcome, and at least half the class had contributed actively to the discussion. It was a good day for me. My efforts were paying off.

I sat in on a few other classes and always left impressed by my colleagues' talent as well as with at least a couple of ideas that I wanted to try in my own classes. And that, I learned, is the key to making these observations useful. When I watched others teach, I needed to focus on just one or two aspects of their teaching. "How can I be like Gina?" led to overwhelming anxiety, but smaller, more concrete questions, like "How does Gina introduce the topic of intelligence testing?" or "How does Gina use small group work in a large lecture class?" gave me valuable insight about how to improve my own teaching.

And that was my only goal — improvement. I was working towards improvement from a very low baseline — survival. Excellence seemed an impossibly long way off. But the thing about the growth mindset is that it quickly becomes a habit. It never occurred to me to stop working on my teaching. Throughout my graduate school years and through my years as an assistant and associate professor, I faithfully attended workshops at the University Center for Excellence in Teaching. I bought books on classroom demonstrations and had an entire shelf of instructor's manuals filled with vivid examples and hands-on classroom exercises to bring esoteric psychological concepts to life. I attended and presented at teaching conferences and retreats. I asked lots of questions and sat in on my colleagues' classes. I combed through my student evaluations at the end of each semester to find what I could improve the next time I taught the course. The negative comments stung, and I sometimes found myself wallowing in the fixed mindset pattern of self-doubt — "I'm just not good at this" — but a week later that had passed, and I started making changes. Just as with the classroom observations, I found the student evaluations most helpful when I focused on improving just a few aspects of my teaching, rather than trying to address every possible negative outcome. I also found that keeping my goals concrete was far more helpful than general intentions to be a better teacher. Resolving to return graded papers more quickly is a nice goal, but blocking off time in your calendar to actually do the grading is far more effective.

By most accounts today, I am considered an excellent teacher. I earned tenure based on excellence in teaching, I've received several awards and recognitions for teaching, I've published and presented on teaching-related topics in journals and conferences with national scope, and I served on the Teaching Committee of the major professional organization in my field. The Teaching Committee's mission statement charged us "to support and enhance quality teaching of Developmental Science in Higher Education." Where to begin? It was overwhelming. We quickly realized that we needed to focus our efforts on one or two concrete initiatives. We decided to start a mentoring program to match up graduate students at large research universities with excellent teachers from around the country who can help them with all the questions they are too scared to ask the people around them. The program launched the next year. It was a good day for me. My efforts are paying off.

Reference

Dweck, C. S. (2006). *Mindset.* New York: Random House.

CHAPTER THIRTEEN

Utilizing Student Feedback to Improve Teaching

Yi Cheng

Having taught at Indiana University South Bend for nearly twenty years, I am still eager to read my students' teaching evaluations for every single course at the end of each semester. One thing I learned from my experience is a contradiction of sorts: good numerical summaries and comments do not always indicate good teaching, even as not-so-good numbers and student criticisms also often indicate that improvement is needed.

The majority of our students are generous in grading their teachers, much more generous than I was in grading their papers. The very first semester I received student teaching evaluations from my first two courses at Indiana University South Bend, there were comments like "well prepared," "very helpful," "really knowledgeable about the subject," "excellent and enthusiastic teacher," and "one of the best math teachers I have ever had." Wow, I was really good! But similar comments were received the second semester, the semester after, and so on. So, I came to the realization that most students are friendly and appreciative of teachers' work. I would be in a fantasy world if I considered myself literally as good as the most positive comments described.

I did receive criticism, especially during the first few years of my teaching. My attitude toward criticism went through several transitions. In my early years of teaching, I made adjustments for some of the criticisms. For instance, when I received comments like "talks too fast" and "not enough office hours," I made adjustments the following semesters by bringing a note card to the classroom that said "talk slow" to remind myself to slow down, and by providing more office hours. But when I read comments like "she did not answer my questions" and "her exam problems are too hard," my first reaction was defensive — there was so much material to teach and I did not have the time to answer their long questions in class. I silently complained and asked questions about what the student should have done. "Why didn't you come to my office hours?" "The exam problems were only hard for you because you had severe math deficiency coming into the class and might not have studied enough."

As I became a more experienced teacher and developed better student-teacher interactions, I understood my students better. When students made comments like "she did not answer my questions," they were mostly truthful. They mentioned how they felt rejected and dissatisfied. For a teacher, being overly defensive is counter-productive. The issue is not that we have to answer all questions raised by students in the classroom; that would be poor class time management. It is about having the answer delivered in a timely and effective manner. Saying "see me after class for answers" is right but might not be enough. Too often, students did not voluntarily come to see me after class even if they were invited. That did not give me any excuse to let it go — "Hey, I made an offer; it's your loss not to come."

A student's loss in learning is our loss in teaching. Judging the situation and the nature of the question, there are various ways to follow up. Sometimes, when I felt that face-to-face communication was necessary to answer the question thoroughly, I invited the students repeatedly, and most of them came after the second or third invitation. More often, when I felt that providing a well-written solution was sufficient, I wrote a detailed step-by-step solution and posted it in the Oncourse course management system, on the same day if possible, at least no later than the second day.

Criticism often carries constructive content. With open and fair minds, we may benefit greatly from criticisms, particularly criticisms from our students that give us first-hand information. Winston Churchill once said: "Criticism may not be agreeable, but it is necessary; it fulfills the same function as pain in the human body, it calls attention to the development of an unhealthy state of things." Some of the most "painful" comments that I received turned out to be the most helpful and most constructive ones.

In my third year teaching at Indiana University South Bend, I had the flu and lost my voice for a week. Not being able to teach, I had another professor cover my classes. At the end of the semester, I received the following comment from a student in my precalculus class:

> Dr. Cheng was too fast in class. I really struggled with the material, even though I went to tutoring with her every single week. The only time I did well on quizzes was when we had a sub from Notre Dame. I think this was because he got the class involved doing problems on the board. He didn't just keep talking and writing. She doesn't ask the class for feedback — she answers everything herself. She's finished writing out a problem and on to the next before a student has the ability to understand

what happened. I'm very unhappy with the way this class was. Everyone was quiet as a graveyard — no questions etc. — except for when we had the sub. I can't learn and grasp concepts this way. Also, many students kept asking to take quizzes before new material was covered and the quiz material was forgotten. Teaching math is hard, I'm sure, but she should maybe think of a new technique for future classes, and listen to her student's ideas.

I would be lying if I said I did not feel unfairly criticized at the very first moment I read it. Looking at the comments and thinking about how much hard work I put into teaching this course, including offering evening and weekend office hours and grading all assignments with detailed corrections, I was holding back tears. How could you call it a "graveyard"? Look at these facts: the student teaching evaluation for the course has a numerical average of 3.53 out of 4, and the majority of students wrote positive comments.

Soon, my good sense and objectivity came back to me. Reading the comment again with a much fairer mind, I realized how sincere the student was. This was a motivated student who was eager to learn and had put great effort into it but was not able to learn effectively with my teaching method. The comment was factual and reasonable. Not only did s/he paint a clear picture of what I did wrong, but s/he also specifically pointed out why I failed and provided the direction of the improvement by comparing my lectures with the sub's lectures. I started looking into the issue, reviewing my lecture notes and analyzing my teaching approach. I came to the painful and truthful conclusion that the student's comment was mostly right and my self-defense was mostly wrong. Yes, I did work hard and made a lot of effort to teach the class "correctly." But so what? Doing my best does not mean much unless I am doing what is necessary and effective for student learning. I was more focused on my own thoughts than on the student's learning preference and what the student needed. "Let's have another example, another equation, another formula, another story problem." My argument was that if I could cover more examples, they would be exposed to more techniques and that would enhance their problem-solving skills. If the students had a quiz at the end of class, they could have a little more time, extending to ten of the fifteen minutes break time between classes. As a result, the pace got faster, the explanations got shorter, the illustrations became vague, and the quiz got longer. Gee, were these all intended to benefit student learning? That was my one-sided self-convincing argument. What was the point of having more examples when my students could not even understand a few?

I consulted the professor who substituted for me, and asked how he did his lectures. As he explained his teaching strategies, he also told me that he mainly used the lecture notes that I provided to him when he taught my class. Even with the same lecture notes, the method of delivering the content can make a big difference. Teaching is a mixture of art and science. I still have a great deal to improve in both areas.

In the course of putting effort into pedagogical change, my emphasis became more centered on effective teaching and student learning. The idea behind having many examples is that it gives students more models to follow. It might be well-intentioned, but it did not lead to good learning outcomes. Lao Tze, an ancient Chinese philosopher, said, "Give a man a fish; feed him for a day. Teach a man to fish; feed him for a lifetime." The "having as many examples as possible" approach gives the students fish, but takes the thinking part out of the assignment and makes students procedural performers, repeating, reciting, but not initiating or fully understanding. As a result, students depend on the teacher to problem-solve for them, which is ineffective and problematic for their skill development and intellectual growth. It takes away the students' responsibility for their own learning and impacts their motivation.

Daily teaching has many pragmatic components, and choosing examples is one of them. Based on student feedback and my own observations, I found that classroom examples should be conceptually representative and operationally simple. "Simple" here does not mean easy or trivial. It means to avoid tedious examples that would take a boatload of class time and shift students' attention to computational or algebraic details rather than conceptual buildup. For a new concept, choosing a starting example as a supporting statement of the concept and plugging appropriate quantities into a formula derived from the concept to get the answer is one way. But while it may be necessary to do this, it may not be sufficient. Engaging students in the derivation of the formula that characterizes the relationship between the quantities not only leads to one useful formula but also enables students to derive new formulas themselves under different scenarios. In Lao Tze's words, "teach a man to fish."

Even with all the appropriate teaching materials, I learned from student feedback that the way of delivering the material can make quite a difference in student learning outcomes. Teaching is an art of conveying knowledge. Communication from different perspectives that are adaptive to diverse learners is crucial. World-renowned musician Yo-Yo Ma once said in a TV interview that, given a piece of music, a cellist should know ten or more different ways to play and to express it. As an instructor, I asked myself: given any concept of mathematics, how many ways can I explain it? Different students have different learning curves and different learning preferences. An explanation that is easy for one type of student to understand may be incomprehensible to others. Even for the students who understood the first explanation, having multiple perspectives about the concept usually helps them understand the concepts with more depth and breadth.

Classroom teaching is only one portion of the teaching process. In all of my classes, there are students who do not grasp the material. Therefore, I always advise my students to use available resources outside the classroom to facilitate learning, such as group studies, tutoring services, Oncourse information, and YouTube lectures.

One important part of teaching outside the classroom is delivered in the instructor's office hours. Nothing can replace the component of office hours for its unique and special functions. In a one-on-one, face-to-face environment I can provide personal attention and differentiated instruction. I can identify individual needs and target specific topics at a specific level. Office-hour instruction and question sessions provide an effective way to help students catch up on concepts that they missed, as well as challenge advanced students to go above and beyond the regular curriculum.

While proactive students tend to use office hours more frequently, many of my students do not use office hours as much as they should. Over the years, I have been consistently encouraging students to come to my office hours and offering appointments, including evenings and weekends when a student could not make my regular office hours.

I never thought that my own attitude during office hours consultations was a problem until one student wrote in the teaching evaluation:

> If you complain about nobody visiting you in your
> office hours then when people visit you, they should

not be made to feel stupid or that their questions do not matter. This is how I felt after coming to see you and that made me lose my confidence I had about the class and I stopped trying thereafter. I might not have the strongest math abilities but I tried and then was let down by your attitude towards the simplest questions. I felt that the questions I asked, you felt [you were] too good to answer. That should be addressed in the future.

The comment was from a student in a probability class. I recognized the event and the issue right after reading the comment. This is what happened. I was teaching course C (Probability) for which course B (Calculus) was the prerequisite. And course A (Precalculus) was the prerequisite for course B. The student came to my office asking questions about course C, and I tried several different ways to answer but they could not understand due to the deficiency in course B. I tried to review the part the student was supposed to learn in course B. The student still could not understand due to deficiency in course A. Ultimately, I realized I had to review the relevant topics covered in course A.

I recalled that as I reviewed the concepts from the prerequisite courses I was quite frustrated, wondering how the student would ever make up the deficiencies and catch up to the current course material. Evidently, my frustration showed even though I did not say a single word about it. The student sensed it and was discouraged; feelings were hurt, and the motivated brain froze. I was insensitive and unprofessional, for which I could not forgive myself. If a student comes to ask a question, a teacher should answer it, ideally until the student can demonstrate understanding by explaining it to the teacher.

Throughout the consultation, the teacher should keep a welcoming style and friendly tone. This is our duty. If we as teachers are less motivated to teach students who have subject matter deficiencies, how can we motivate students to learn? Clearly, the student is already frustrated, and adding to the frustration only alienates the student. For its impact on student learning outcomes, our positive attitudes matter as much as our effective teaching skills.

Being sensitive to the needs of students is an important quality of a good teacher. Pedagogical frameworks derived from educational psychology and cognitive psychology are powerful tools that can help us foster better understanding of our students and their learning process. Every student is different with his/her unique personality and learning preferences. I learned from this experience that it is important that I have a good appreciation for my students' academic abilities and capabilities and that I remain sensitive to their strengths and weaknesses. Develop patience and compassion. Be versatile in communication in order to interact with all types of students effectively. Build mutual trust so students will not hesitate to ask for help when needed. Such trust plays an important role in student learning.

A few years ago, I was stuck at Chicago O'Hare Airport for several hours due to weather conditions and ran into one of my colleagues at Indiana University South Bend. She is well known at our campus for her dedication to student service, particularly student advising. We chatted for more than three hours (quality time) about teaching and advising. We shared many common thoughts, including this one: students know their teachers much more than we give them credit for. If a teacher genuinely cares about student learning, they know. If a teacher does not care as much, they know. If a teacher talks about caring but does little to prove it, they also know. The list could go on.

Students judge teaching by relevancy and by the impact on their learning. In a football game, passing a football without a reception is an incomplete pass. The same thing can be said about teaching and learning. In this regard, student feedback, particularly criticism, provides a constructive path for us to see our shortfalls and to make improvements.

CHAPTER FOURTEEN

Lessons from Unexpected Teachers

Patricia Lewis

"They won't even ask a question!" I lamented. "My students seem almost afraid to talk, let alone ask a question about solving equations! Some just stare off into space." I needed help learning how to teach. I was at a Special Olympics swim session talking with my friend who was not only the coordinator for these amazing athletes, but also a Special Education teacher.

"You'll get it," she encouraged. "It just takes time to get to know your students."

One of the athletes chimed in, "Sometimes math is hard — maybe you should talk about something else!"

Wow. Light bulbs flashed! Bells and whistles sounded! As the Hallelujah Chorus of Angels played in my head, I wondered at the intelligent simplicity of this answer. This is one of the best pieces of advice that I had gotten! Many students are nervous the first few days of class, and in math and science courses anxiety can run even higher. My students didn't "know me from Adam," so why should they trust me?

This was not the first time I had been amazed by my friends with special needs, and it would be the first of three insights that dramatically impacted the way I taught others. Indeed, I have found that the patient, thoughtful, and creative opinions of those with physical and mental disabilities are gems that are often overlooked in our society. With renewed insight, I began to plan my math class.

The next day, there were no pre-written notes on the board, just me, sitting there with a smile (a nervous smile — but a smile nonetheless!). "Today, we are going to get to know one another," I said. "So, starting in the first row I would like you to tell me your name, your major, and one other fact about you — anything! It could be how many kids you have; it could be that you just went skydiving or maybe one of your hobbies — anything." Within forty-five minutes I got to know my students a little better, and conversations ensued.

Once I started my lecture, I knew most names and received a few smiles. Then the miraculous happened. A lone hand raised into the air! I struggled to remember the name, the student prompted me, and we had a discussion. I asked if the student understood my answer — and the student did! Yes! A mechanical engineer by background, I was learning to become a successful teacher.

My second major insight began several weeks later, when we had our first exam in math class. Despite the trust and communication we had built, I found that not all of my students were with me — a few did poorly on the test. I was stumped. They were asking questions, weren't they? Hadn't I reached them?

At the same time, we were going to parent-teacher conferences for my two oldest children. Our first-grade daughter, Danielle, had started reading at the early age of three, prompted by her older sister "playing school," but we were concerned because she was clearly not understanding what was being asked of her while testing. If we went over the material with her auditorially, she seemed to grasp it much more quickly and with better retention. We suspected a learning disability.

The response of her teacher is still emblazoned in my mind. "Not all children can excel. Your daughter, for example, is simply an underachiever and probably just a B or C student. Perhaps if she stopped staring off into space."

I was dumbfounded. This conference would change my perspective on education forever.

After excusing our daughter from the room, we told this teacher of the mismatch between Danielle's early reading start and the diagnosis of being "just a B or C" student. We spoke of students living up (or down) to expectations. Finally, we expressed our disappointment that a teacher would openly label a student, with the student present.

We returned home, determined to help our daughter succeed but without much guidance on what we should do. This experience sparked me to do some research. I was soon chatting with education faculty and students about how best to help students learn. Pursuing a Master's in Liberal Arts allowed me to study learning disabilities and linear equations, educational assessments and algebra.

Sitting in a graduate education class one evening, I was surprised to hear that my professor was dyslexic and had thought himself stupid until he got to college! Although he had two PhDs in Education and Special Education, and had won numerous teaching awards, he had not read remedial material until second grade. Symbols and signs often flipped around in math and science courses. Historically a "C" or below student, he loved to talk, though his teachers tried to get him to work quietly.

He shared a particularly troubling habit. "When I did not understand material, I would stare off into space. It was as if I was zoning out. I would get yelled at for daydreaming and worse yet — cheating. But now we know that this is an indication of an auditory learner and possible dyslexia. These periods of staring are when the mind is racing, trying to catch up with the material and seeking any other clues."

When he reached college and could use study groups, a light bulb went on! This material was easy. He understood it. He could explain it to others. He told us, "I joined every study group available!"

That day a light bulb went on for me as well. My child was dyslexic. She was trying to process material that was not presented in a format that she could easily absorb. (Testing later proved that this was indeed the case!) We went crazy with the auditory methods. Books on tape were requested. If they were not available, we recorded them ourselves. Spelling words were recited into a tape recorder and played back again and again. Math and science were more difficult to modify. Unless she was allowed to "dialogue" a problem, it was harder for her to catch her mistakes.

Wait just a second . . . could these techniques help my students as well? Were some of them auditory learners who might have more trouble with the more visual subjects of math and science?

My seven-year-old dyslexic child was teaching me how to teach! I dove into research on learning disabilities and the three main learning styles. My graduate capstone project paired this research with mathematics. Visual learners have it the easiest! They learn by viewing material and are better able to reproduce it later, and the majority of traditional teaching techniques are visual and play to their strengths. The other two types of learners, tactile (hands on) and auditory learners, do not have this advantage. In fact, in math and science, they are at a distinct disadvantage.

I gave a learning style assessment to my students. For comparison of data, I looked at their previous math course scores. My engineering mode kicked in and I was soon doing correlation studies and constructing graphs. If I could find the problem, perhaps I could fix it.

Sure enough, the majority of my students were auditory or tactile learners. Those who were visual learners were achieving higher scores in my class as well as previous ones. So what could be done? I know that my daughters both had high IQs and differing learning styles. We were slowly finding ways to help my younger one express her true knowledge on exams.

Well . . . whatever worked for my younger daughter, I would try in my classroom! We had found that extra time and the ability to "talk aloud" to herself while testing were key. So I doubled the testing time in my class. If some were still not finished, I stayed even later. I noticed many of them moving their mouths while testing. I offered these students the chance to sit in the hall or a nearby room, and talk to themselves.

Another technique that seemed to help was the use of colors. I would use them in breaking things down for my daughter — why not my class? I used color coding to identify which pieces of equations went together. Students could follow the path of directions by combining same-colored terms.

What a difference a rainbow can make! As my hands grew into multi-colored clouds of chalk, my students solved equations, many with a pack of colored pencils in hand.

Grading the next exam was a lot more fun — the answers were correct! And better yet, the methods were understood. Once students were given the time and a method that worked for them, they were able to express their true potential. Once again, a person with a learning difference, my own child, had been my teacher.

But God wasn't done with me yet — oh no! I had so much more to learn about teaching, and the third lesson was going to be a doozy!

By this time, I was teaching at Indiana University South Bend. I had gotten to know the Office of Disability Support Services quite well. I had developed the "rep" that I could and would work with challenged students.

It was Fall term. I remember clearly the hot August sun and the brilliant flowers as I hurried to cross the walkway into the Technology building. I was trying to be early to get a jump on introductions. My classes each term were usually full with a long waitlist, which made me smile because it meant that I was doing a good job. But it also made my task a bit harder, having a classroom at or above capacity. This class was full — plus one! The math department had asked me to allow an extra student in, one who had requested accommodations. I took attendance and went over the syllabus, telling students that if they did need special accommodations, they could give me the letter now or in private after class.

Five or six people waved their white envelopes at me, seeming very comfortable with their request for help. We went through my now routine "name game" for introductions, then it was time to dismiss class. As they poured out of the room, I noticed a stylish woman who stayed seated by the window. She smiled in my direction as I tried to recall her name.

"Do you have a question?" I asked, "Anne, isn't it?"

"Yes, I'm Anne Drake, and I wanted to talk with you about accommodations."

"Well, that is usually done with the Office of Disability Support Services, and then you bring me the list of your needs."

"Well, I am not sure if I have needs. I am not sure that I can even take this class let alone pass it!"

"Oh, Anne! Of course you can! I have taught many students with disabilities, and I can truly say that the only one who I felt could not master this class was a lady who was borderline mentally impaired — and I say that with utmost sincerity, as she was in Special Olympics."

Anne smiled and reached into her purse and started unwrapping a stick. No, it was a cane. A white cane with a red tip. I thought — "how can I ask her about her obvious visual impairment?" I was unsure how to approach this.

"Anne, stupid question."

"Mrs. Lewis, you said that there are no stupid questions and I think I know what you're about to ask me."

"Wow, good to know someone was listening to me."

"Yes, I am slowly losing my vision and am now legally blind. I have a small amount of vision left. So yes! I listen very well."

"Deep breaths, Tricia," I told myself, "deep breaths before you talk." So, here was my next "teacher." And wow, what a lesson plan!

"OK, Anne, please let me know how I can help you. I am new to this, but I think you and I will do just fine. When was the last time you had math, and how did you do? Did you like it?"

"Wow, you don't waste time do you?" Anne said. I liked her. Anne Drake had much more than style, she had moxie. If she was willing to give it a shot, then so was I.

I called the Indiana University South Bend Office of Disability Support Services to ask them how soon they could get our textbook transferred to a Daisy reader, which is a book reader designed to help the visually impaired. I had learned of this during my struggles to have my daughter's books put on tape. The magnitude of my challenge went from a ski hill to Mount Everest, as they responded with "book on what"? I explained about my new student and once again requested that her book be put into a mode that she could listen to. I was again met with silence.

I was put on hold for a few minutes and was then told, "We recommend that you call our Bloomington office. We have never had a blind student. We simply do not have the equipment." My father suggested that I call the Indiana School for the Blind in Indianapolis. I learned that Braille for math and science is a special kind, called Nemeth code, and Anne was not at that point yet.

Their advice did come in handy in regards to teaching methods. The books that I was sent stressed a clear, concise speaking voice, as well as vocalizing each and every mark that I wrote on the blackboard. Huh, this was going to take some effort on my part. I speak quickly and by that I mean "speed racer." Anne was going to have to slow me down.

What a perfect match! Anne's openness about her situation made the class a better learning environment and me a better instructor. She would often ask to have things repeated. Students understood that the noise in the room needed to be minimal so that Anne could hear. Other students often responded if I asked for a re-statement of the method. We had a community.

We have applied this concept to a new type of class at Indiana University South Bend. In Fall semester of 2009, I was asked to help develop a "pilot" community class for our introductory level algebra. The most important aspect that I emphasized with my input was to create a sense of support. This course, A100, is set up in groups. The students work at tables so that they can interact. From day one, we require the students to vocalize their concerns. They may ask me, an in-room tutor, or their tablemates for help. We want them to feel comfortable in the classroom.

Community. That's just what I had started out to achieve so many years before in my first teaching experience. Each time that I added more effort to bring this to my classroom, students thrived that much more. We all enjoyed being there. Math class was something that students actually looked forward to! By the third semester that Anne was enrolled in my classes, the students had approached the university about a teaching award for me. As part of this process, I was asked to write an analysis and theory of teaching. I had never really sat down before to figure that out. What did I believe? What truly worked with college students?

The university talked of retention. They touted the fact that the number of students who passed my class and went on to be successful in others was quite high. I was asked to give input with a seminar on "bottleneck" courses and how we help students to excel beyond them. Though I was flattered that my numbers were recognized, I wanted to know why I was successful. Retention is great — but why and how were we retaining some students and losing others? What was it that helped students to succeed?

It was and is my strongest belief that instructors should feel a sense of ownership in their students' education. They should revel in student success and feel culpable in their failures. I wanted my students to know that I would support them if they put in an equal effort. I wanted my students to feel that I was a part of their community.

Instructors should promote a sense of community. The seed for this idea was planted with the advice from a Special Olympics athlete. It had grown and developed through a very personal journey with my own daughter, Danielle. Finally it had bloomed with the help of Ms. Anne Drake, who now has a master's degree in social work.

Through their willingness to share their special needs, these three amazing individuals taught me to meet the needs of my students. They helped me to understand how others might feel. They showed me that, though students might have differing needs, these needs might be a strength. Finally, they showed me that embracing all learning styles in a classroom can make it into a community where students help each other. These three "teachers" will forever be in my heart.

CHAPTER FIFTEEN

Finding Myself

Sara Sage

"We teach who we are."
    - Parker Palmer, *The Courage to Teach*

EDUC F201/F202, *Exploring the Personal Demands of Teaching Laboratory and Field Experience*, has a more than thirty-five-year history at Indiana University South Bend. This course, which essentially is about, and is taught from, the humanistic declaration of Parker Palmer given above, has been a constant companion on my own journey of growth as a teacher and human being for my past nineteen years at Indiana University South Bend. I see that my own path, which began from a place I might call "I must be right as the expert," has meandered on to a place I currently name "I must be my authentic self."

Before I begin my own story, I would like to share a few words about the history of this course. Three years ago, as part of my full-year sabbatical research, I interviewed Randy Isaacson, who essentially brought the course to Indiana University South Bend as an adaptation of a course that he had taught as a graduate assistant at Michigan State University on affective education, and Vince Peterson, who contributed to the course from a humanistic counseling perspective and taught the course, as did other counseling faculty, for many years. Vince offered the perspective that the primary goal of preparing teachers was for them to be able to demonstrate an authentic relationship with their students that involved seeing each student as a person, being able to listen, and including that emotional component in the classroom. The F201 course emphasized skills from Thomas Gordon's work, *Teacher Effectiveness Training*, and much was based on Carl Rogers's person-centered approach. Randy shared how he was hired partly to bring more structure to the teaching of educational psychology and, in the process, brought this new F201 course. He emphasized how his approach to the course has changed over the years from focusing only on care and compassion to expanding the focus into teacher leadership and the importance of being assertive and being able to give negative feedback so that teachers have the "backbone" they need to address unprofessionalism and difficult issues in today's schools.

When I was hired at Indiana University South Bend for the fall of 1997, and Floyd Urbach, then the Chair of Secondary Education, asked me what I wanted to teach for my first semester, I jumped at the chance to teach the F201 course. I had never taught anything like it, but I had been fascinated by how K-12 teachers teach and who they are as people and teachers since my first years as a special education teacher. When I talked with K-12 general education teachers about including my students with visual impairments and learning disabilities in their classrooms and planned with them, I was intrigued by how easy it was with some teachers and how difficult with others. My teaching lens at the time was the Myers-Briggs Type Indicator, and I could see that teachers who were ISFJs, for example, often seemed to have more predictable instructional events for which my instructional aide and I could Braille materials ahead of time. On the other hand, a notable ENFP teacher who was one of the most welcoming to my young blind students, was also notorious for deciding five minutes before they came to the classroom to do something different. In this classroom, my students were often included enthusiastically but without materials in Braille to read. Another first grade teacher (probably ISTJ) couldn't seem to allow my first-grade low-vision student to sit up on his haunches on his desk and put his nose practically right down on the paper to read it, because the rule was: Sit on your bottom in your desk. That made no sense to me.

So I explored teachers and professional development further in my M.A. and Ph.D. programs in Curriculum, Instruction, and Professional Development at Ohio State University in a wonderful mix of experiences in teacher education, psychology, and the affective realm, such as job-embedded professional development, stages of teacher development, Jungian theory, and adult development theory. Then I worked for several years at the Illinois Mathematics and Science Academy doing research and training K-12 teachers in problem-based learning (PBL). Again, it was fascinating to me to watch not only how my colleagues and I worked differently in workshops but also how we needed to work differently with different teachers.

It was also an educative but painful experience to see how I could work while going through a divorce, custody issues, and a major move from Chicago to South Bend as a single parent to begin a brand new faculty position. As a result, I was a wounded soul when I began my first semester and taught F201 for the first time. I had difficulty being kind to myself, and I certainly had difficulty confronting students who were not meeting standards. I remember an incident in class when one male student spilled coffee accidentally on a female student's coat sleeve, and she went ballistic. When I commented to her after class about practicing some of our class skills like using "I" messages and active listening, she said, "But why should I? That was personal." I had no idea what to say to her. Everything seemed to rub salt in my wounds those days, and I often took things personally myself.

After a few years, my son and I had settled into the South Bend area, and I began to do some healing. At that point, I adapted the F201 course syllabus and some of the assignments to ones that were working well for me. We began doing a PBL experience in the course where students worked together in small groups, as simulated middle school teaching teams, to create their "back to school" team newsletter to parents. This activity generated conflict in the small groups — which was my goal — but I was often at a loss with how to facilitate and process it for student learning. One semester was particularly difficult. I had a secondary education major, a female, in the class, who was very aggressive and felt that the course curriculum was asking her to change her personality. This is not an unusual response to the more humanistic view of interacting with others promoted in the course, but I could sense that this student simply thought I was wrong and, although I knew that underneath she was scared and experiencing some "I'm not good enough" thoughts, she was very difficult to deal with, openly challenging me in class. I had a hard time being assertive enough to call her on it, or to accept it and talk about it, and ended up writing one of our School of Education "letters of concern" about teacher candidate dispositions, or affective issues, at the end of the semester. She hit the ceiling, wrote me an incredibly personal and negative evaluation, and was certainly spreading the bad word about me in a variety of places, including online. I was once again wounded and felt perhaps similar to her underneath — that I wasn't good enough to teach this class.

The next semester, I was given a teaching gift. I had an amazingly open and growth-oriented F201 class. I had a delightful young woman in class in whom I could see an incredible amount of leadership potential but who could not yet see it in herself. I placed her in the role of the middle-school team chairperson, and she had to direct her group through the collaboration and writing process. After the first class session of the project, she stayed after class and burst into tears because she felt like a failure for allowing another more assertive student in her group to direct the process. I counseled her through her concerns, stating again that I was confident she could be a good leader and that leadership could often look like facilitating, rather than directing, and allowing a process to work. As I was beginning to trust my own process of growing and learning as a faculty member and a teacher, I could begin to extend this same trust to my students. Her group ended up creating a very effective parent newsletter, and our debriefing session at the end of the project remains, to this day, one of my most memorable moments as a teacher, when this student talked at length about what she learned about herself as a leader and others listened intently and supported her. Just when I felt "redeemed" from the previous semester's disaster, during one of my end-of-semester one-on-one conferences with the students, I heard from a quiet, introverted student that another student had bullied her in class by rolling her eyes whenever the first student talked and was talking negatively about her outside of class. I had missed the whole thing in my need to feel better about what was going on. Once again, I felt like a failure.

In the twelve years or so since then, I have gotten tenure and promotion to associate professor, graduated my son from high school to college and into adulthood and marriage, and earned a master's degree in mental health counseling right here on my own campus as a student (while simultaneously being a faculty member), which was an interesting balance of dual relationships with colleagues who became my teachers. I participated in several *Courage to Teach* and *Living from Within* groups in Michigan, based on the work of Parker Palmer. These circles helped me learn to be quiet, to reflect, to listen, and to renew my dedication to my vocation as a teacher and to accept my new joint vocation as a counselor. In the middle of the counseling program, in 2007, my mother got a terminal cancer diagnosis and died within four months. During that semester, when I was doing the minimum possible at Indiana University South Bend and driving to southwestern lower Michigan almost every day to be with my mother and father, my students were so loving and respectful. Somehow I felt I had developed into a human being who was more concerned with being loving and respectful than always being right or being the most competent, and I saw that reflected back from my students.

My work as a counseling intern and now as a licensed mental health counselor here in North Central Indiana has made me so much more aware of the pain and stress so many of our students go through and how much hunger there is in our world for non-judgment, a safe "container" to provide people in order to do their own good work, and simply someone to listen and accept people where they are. I also have finally learned some of those confronting skills and how to do them in a safe, non-threatening, and assertive way with students. Now, I typically do not fear any student coming into F201, because I know we will be working with each other in an authentic relationship. Like my now deceased mentor Vince Peterson, I simply remain curious about how to work with the student effectively as opposed to dreading it or being afraid. Additionally, like my recently retired mentor Randy Isaacson, I have become unwilling to accept anything less than excellence in my students and often gently but firmly challenge them through feedback and encouragement to work harder to give something their best. On a very practical note, being a student again reminded me of how important it is that I actually use my chosen textbooks well, how practical and useful my assignments should be, and how useless and offensive busy work is to adult learners.

As I become more devoted to a path of compassion and respect following both Native American and Buddhist traditions, I am able to be more myself — more authentic — and to be more available and present with students in F201 and other classes. What I see happening now in my teaching is a process that allows students to bring their whole selves to the class, including their biases, their stressors, their tragedies, their fears, and their blind spots — all of which are wonderful and all of which now provide me with much more authentic class discussions and interactions, with accompanying tensions, conflicts, controversial discussions, and rich wisdom. This new welcoming of dark and light topics in my classes has stretched my teaching skills to include most of the counseling skills I am developing as well as new skills in leading discussions, asking questions, and balancing depth with breadth in the curriculum. It is still not easy when I have a student whose "dispositions" for teaching are rough, or when I make the difficult professional judgment that a particular student is just not prepared to become a teacher at this time. I am learning to trust my judgment, and I do my best to be honest with such students and help them develop a plan for growth or consider other career options. I am learning how to listen to my own inner wisdom as I teach, listen, assess, and grow. I have reached that "certain age" where, as one of my friends said, you turn and face your tribe and say, "Here I am — this is who I am and what I have to offer" (with an unspoken "take it or leave it"!).

I began this reflection with one of my favorite quotes from *The Courage to Teach*, in which Parker Palmer simply states: "We teach who we are." I am the same person I was nineteen years ago, but with very different understandings and a much richer diversity of personal experiences, strengths, and skills on which to draw as a teacher. I can see how my students respond to my same but richer self, and I am again renewed in my calling to prepare teachers who are rich and self-aware human beings, who reflect on the importance of relationship and acceptance with their students, and who reflect on themselves in a broad variety of ways as they grow as people and teachers.

CHAPTER SIXTEEN

Reaching Out, Building Bridges

P. N. Saksena

I am living a blessed life. I have had the honor and privilege of walking into the classroom and instructing students for more than two decades, while having fun and the satisfaction of being able to reach them. It is particularly gratifying, since I am at a teaching-first institution and have had numerous wonderful opportunities to interact with and influence a number of hard-working first-generation college students. I have seen them mature, start their jobs, marry and start a family, and advance in their careers. It is always a pleasure to run into students around town and just catch up.

My unlikely journey to Indiana University South Bend started in New Delhi, India. I decided to major in business in my junior year of high school. After one year of undergraduate education, I found the pace excruciatingly slow and felt that I did not connect with my teachers. Without meaningful advice and mentorship, I decided to hasten my pace and accomplish as much as I could. While pursuing my undergraduate degree via correspondence, I was also working on my accounting certification and starting a job. Four years went by quickly, but I had accomplished a lot: completed my undergraduate degree, acquired my accounting certification, gained experience in public and managerial accounting, and, best of all, got married.

Shortly thereafter, my wife and I were fortunate to come to the US to continue my education.

At the University of Georgia, I was surrounded by some faculty members whom I characterized as passionate in their field, who loved teaching, and who were able to reach out to students in a friendly way. Through the years, I noticed their unique ability to build bridges with their students. I was fortunate to have opportunities to teach. Teaching was both exhilarating and rewarding, particularly because my students responded to my efforts and appreciated my reaching out to them. It became so much clearer to me the special value of being mindful to reach out to students, to build bridges, and, in the process, celebrate their academic accomplishments.

During this time, I was happy to be completing my master's degree. Earning a Ph.D. in accounting was not even on my radar. However, the indescribable feeling I got when I was teaching and the support I received from my professors made me realize that I could do more things with a doctorate. Those passionate faculty members not only inspired me, but also supported me in my new journey as a doctoral student.

A short seventy-mile move in Georgia, and I was enrolled in an accounting doctoral program. Once again I was blessed to be in the company of faculty members who genuinely cared about their students. While I was a student, I was a keen observer of what effective instruction should and could be. Increasingly, I realized that one of the most important skills is the ability to build bridges, to connect with students, and to reach them in ways that support their academic careers. I was reminded of this consistently as both a student and a teaching assistant.

As a student myself, I realized that students, in general, valued and respected the professor and flourished in their own learning when the professor genuinely cared about them and was respectful of them. I also realized that this was possible when the instructor used several strategies to reach students. There really was no one-size-fits-all strategy that worked for all students.

It was fortuitous to work as an assistant professor at Indiana University South Bend shortly after graduation. Our goals aligned — that is, teaching first. As a faculty member in the School of Business and Economics, I found a dedicated faculty whose colleagues from other schools and colleges also had the same long history of being effective in the classroom. Better yet, they were open to sharing their "secrets," and the institution made a commitment to excellence in teaching. This gave me an opportunity to interact with dedicated and committed faculty members whose mantra seemed to be "continuous improvement."

As my teaching started in earnest, I was reminded of the importance of building bridges to reach students. I employed several strategies. For example, I explained why I covered certain topics in class, why I pushed students to master the material, why I sought input about what worked for them and what didn't through midterm evaluations. Throughout, I communicated openly, honestly, and regularly with students, sharing my home/cell phone number, etc. I also gained experience in a number of areas of accounting, both at the graduate and undergraduate levels, and employed appropriate strategies to continue to build bridges.

In 2008, I decided to add flexibility to my graduate classes by offering them in a hybrid format. This came about through comments from students in my midterm evaluations. Graduate students appreciated the in-class interactions; however, they asked for flexibility as a way for them to better balance their work and personal lives. Since I have always enjoyed new strategies and pedagogies/androgogies in my classes I added periodic online classes and ventured into the hybrid format.

While students had requested it, there was significant concern on their part as far as periodic online classes were concerned. After an extensive discussion and step-by-step instructions, we tried our first online class. There were a few issues that were ironed out after some discussion, and ideas were shared openly in class. I found that a hybrid class worked well in continuing to reach my students. Students were also able to establish and maintain relationships with their peers and with me. I have continued to use this model with success and on a consistent basis for many of my classes. In fact, we worked on and are now offering our redesigned MBA program in a hybrid format.

Things progressed well, and, in spring 2009, I had the opportunity to develop a fully online course that I would teach in the fall semester that year. Indiana University South Bend had made a commitment to distance/online education, and I wanted to join the innovative group of faculty teaching online courses. I developed and taught an undergraduate managerial accounting online course in fall 2009. Course development involved gaining a better understanding of using both computer hardware and software programs that enhanced my teaching. It was an important learning curve. I noticed that some of the instructional strategies that I successfully implemented in my face-to-face courses were not as successful in my online or hybrid courses. It was apparent that I had to revisit my strategies, particularly when I taught my first online course.

I had three face-to-face meetings with students, and the rest was online. The first class was held face-to-face so I could discuss the structure of the online course with students. I wanted my students to know what they could expect of me and what I expected of them.

I also wanted them to ask questions and to have a sense of how the class would progress throughout the semester.

The semester started well, and things were progressing satisfactorily, a fact that was borne out by student comments on the midterm evaluation (a tool I have used throughout my teaching career). However, I was surprised when I received the final course evaluations. Up to this point in my teaching career, I had been successful in building bridges to reach my students, whether it was in my face-to-face classes or hybrid classes. Additionally, I felt I had done my best to reach out to students in the online class. I realized, in reviewing students' feedback, I had been unsuccessful in connecting with students in this class as meaningfully as I had in my other classes. This realization was troubling, but it motivated me to find and implement strategies that would work in an online environment and connect me with students in a meaningful way.

While I was available via several modes, including in person, phone (office and cell), e-mail, videoconferencing, and our learning management system, I realized that I had failed to make students feel that I was in class with them, that I supported them, and that I celebrated their accomplishments through papers, exams, discussion forum postings, and other activities. In many significant ways, I was not as attentive to the needs of students who were on the fence, who were getting lost, or who did not reach out to me. I erroneously assumed that my giving them opportunities to speak with me would be enough to build a successful and meaningful bridge.

I learned a lot from my first online experience, and, because I had a lot of questions and ideas, I reached out to experts and willing colleagues across campus who had significant experience in developing and teaching online classes. This helped me implement different strategies the next time. For instance, I used the discussion forums more effectively, posing questions that students could answer with some degree of reflection and analysis. I was constantly monitoring students' postings and responding to them in a timely manner. I also made sure that students were interacting with me and with each other often and respectfully. I regularly reminded them to reach out to me either directly or through the Forums tool in our learning management system. Additionally, I created a unique thread for each week through which I reminded students that I was available and ready to assist and support them in their online learning experience.

As I have continued to teach, I have remained vigilant in finding effective ways to build bridges and to reach out to my students, irrespective of the format used. I have come to the realization that each course delivery medium is unique and it is imperative to give special attention to the techniques used to reach out to students.

As I reflect on what strategies I implemented that successfully supported me in reaching out to students and building bridges, I highlight my top three, which apply to face-to-face, hybrid, and online courses.

1. *Pay attention to each student's progress in class.* When someone doesn't seem to be submitting assignments that reflect clear understanding of the subject matter, I email or call that student to either come see or speak with me over the phone, video-conference system, or whatever technological tool I can rely on to ensure that I am able to discuss the student's challenges, goals, etc. This way, I can come up with some kind of intervention that could motivate him or her to do better in the course.

2. *Actively listen not only to what students are saying but also to what they are not saying.* There are several opportunities in an on-campus or online class when students are able to articulate

what they have learned and what they are still grappling with. However, for students who are quiet or not actively participating in group projects, for example, I really try to find out what's going on with them by talking to them after class or online and even through text messages. I have found that this kind of reaching out has made my students feel that I deeply care for them.

3. Help students feel that I had similar struggles when I was in school and that I was able to transcend them. Not only making the content of my course real to my students but also telling them about my own personal struggles and those of others in an authentic way helps them regard me as a person and not some kind of superhero. Somehow I found that my vulnerability made me less intimidating to them, and they feel more comfortable in expressing themselves in a meaningful and respectful way. In many ways, I am able to provide them with what they could perceive as a safe space to learn.

Reach out and build bridges — that is the lesson I have learned and what I will always strive to do in many aspects of my professional and personal life.

Acknowledgements

Any book is first and foremost a collaborative effort. The editors would like to thank the authors who took the time to write their narratives. We extend our deepest gratitude to each of them for sharing their experiences and, in many ways, their teaching souls.

- Jannette (Joy) Alexander, Associate Professor Emeritus of Counseling and Human Services
- Elizabeth Bennion, Professor of Political Science
- Rebecca Brittenham, Professor of English
- Anne Brown, Professor of Mathematical Sciences
- Yi Cheng, Professor of Mathematical Sciences
- Alfred J. Guillaume, Jr., Professor Emeritus of French and Former Executive Vice Chancellor for Academic Affairs
- Neovi Karakatsanis, Professor of Political Science
- Harold (Tuck) Langland, Professor Emeritus of Sculpture
- Patricia Lewis, Associate Faculty of Mathematical Sciences
- Gwendolyn (Gwynn) Mettetal, Chancellor's Professor of Psychology and Education
- Carolyn Schult, Associate Professor of Psychology
- Sara Sage, former Associate Professor of Secondary Education
- P. N. Saksena, former Professor of Accounting
- Monica Tetzlaff, Associate Professor of History
- James (Jay) VanderVeen, Associate Professor of Anthropology and Sociology
- Tom Vander Ven, Professor Emeritus of English

Notes:

Dr. Joy Alexander wrote a narrative as an homage to her mentor, Dr. Vince Peterson, who received a teaching award but passed on before completing his narrative.

Dr. Alfred Guillaume, Jr.'s narrative is included here as the then Executive Vice Chancellor for Academic Affairs when this publication started.

Awards

All-IU Awards:
- Frederick Bachman Lieber Memorial Award
- Herman Frederic Lieber Memoral Award
- Sylvia E. Bowman Award
- President's Award
- Part-time Teaching Award
- Faculty Academy on Excellence in Teaching (FACET)
-

IU South Bend Awards:
- IU South Bend Chancellor's Professor
- Eldon F. Lundquist Award
- IU South Bend Distinguished Teaching Award
- IU South Bend Associate Faculty Distinguished Teaching Award
- IU South Bend Legacy Award
- Trustees' Teaching Award (formerly Teaching Excellence Recognition Award)

All-IU Awards

The Frederic Bachman Lieber Memorial Award, Herman Frederic Lieber Memorial Award, Sylvia E. Bowman Award, President's Award, and Part-Time Teaching Award
These awards are given to call attention to the importance of teaching as well as to recognize those who have demonstrated excellence in a wide range of pedagogical activities. One of each of these awards is given each year.

Faculty Academy on Excellence in Teaching (FACET)

The IU Faculty Academy on Excellence in Teaching, or FACET, is a community of faculty at IU dedicated to and recognized for excellence in teaching and learning. It is a means to provide networking and programs that support the scholarship of teaching and learning. FACET is a unique organization at IU that brings together faculty from all eight campuses. Approximately fifteen faculty are inducted each year.

IU South Bend Awards

Chancellor's Professorship

The Chancellor's Professorship honors a full professor or librarian with highly meritorious performance in all areas of faculty or librarian work. It recognizes a record of extensive accomplishment and leadership in teaching, research, and campus service. The title acknowledges that the breadth and depth of those contributions are vital to the overall success of campus goals and advancement. One award is given each year.

The Eldon F. Lundquist Award

The Lundquist award is made to a meritorious faculty member of Indiana University, South Bend campus, who has exhibited excellence in teaching, scholarly or artistic achievement, and diversified relevant service, preferably in community service throughout the Michiana region. One award is given each year.

IU South Bend Distinguished Teaching Award

The Distinguished Teacher has a consistent and long-standing record of outstanding teaching performance, implementing effective and innovative teaching techniques that demonstrate the unique ability to motivate student learning. One award is given each year.

IU South Bend Associate Faculty Distinguished Teaching Award

The Associate Faculty Distinguished Teacher has a consistent and long-standing record of outstanding teaching performance, implementing effective and innovative teaching techniques that demonstrate the unique ability to motivate student learning. One award is given each year.

IU South Bend Legacy Award

The Legacy Award was established by the IU South Bend Alumni Association to recognize a faculty member for making a difference in the lives of students. One award is given each year.

Trustees' Teaching Award, formerly Teaching Excellence Recognition Award

These awards are given to those applicants who show evidence of sustained and consistent teaching excellence. These annual awards are given to a maximum of 7 percent of the faculty on each campus.

Author Bios

Jannette (Joy) Alexander, Associate Professor Emeritus of Counseling and Human Services, wanted to learn, and so she taught. As a licensed psychologist, she taught counseling courses at IU South Bend for twenty-three years. An Indiana University Teaching Excellence Recognition awardee, she graduated from teaching at IU South Bend and is on her way to the wider world to learn much more. Her curriculum will include being wisdom rather than merely speaking about wisdom. She will continue to share wisdom and much more, teaching and learning at the same time.

Elizabeth Bennion is Professor of Political Science and teaches courses in American politics and political behavior. Her research, teaching, and service focus on civic education and engagement. She is co-editor of the books *Teaching Civic Engagement: From Student to Active Citizen* and *Teaching Civic Engagement Across the Disciplines*. She is also co-founder of the Intercampus Consortium for Scholarship for Teaching and Learning (SoTL) Research. In addition to working with students to host candidate debates, public issue forums, and other civic education events across Michiana, she hosts *Politically Speaking*, a weekly television program on WNIT public television, where she engages students as research and production assistants. She is an eight-time recipient of IU's Trustees' Teaching Award. She also received the Alumni Association's Legacy Award and the Eldon Lundquist Award. In 2011, the South Bend Common Council passed a resolution "Publicly commending IUSB Professor Elizabeth Bennion who serves our community through her excellence in teaching, student-faculty interaction, and collaboration in lifelong learning." She also received both statewide (Indiana Campus

Compact) and national (American Association of State Colleges and Universities) faculty awards for outstanding contributions in the area of civic education. Committed to civic identity formation, she engages all four of her children in service projects and takes them to the polls on Election Day.

Rebecca Brittenham is a Professor of English and most often serves as the Director of First-Year Writing. The majority of her courses focus on the study, practice, and teaching of writing, with occasional sorties into the politics and poetics of food and Victorian ghosts, psychics, and blood-sucking vampires. She is a proud member of the Faculty Colloquium on Excellence in Teaching and has received Indiana University's Frederic Bachman Lieber Memorial Award for Teaching Excellence, the Indiana University South Bend Distinguished Teacher Award, and an Indiana University Trustees' Teaching Award. So far she has graded approximately 1,458,934 papers since coming to IU South Bend in 1998. At night she dreams about food, mostly buffets.

Anne Brown is a Professor of Mathematical Sciences, teaching a range of mathematics courses for future teachers, and for mathematics and other science majors. Her research focuses on the mathematical thinking of college students and on using literacy strategies in mathematics instruction. Besides teaching, she enjoys photography, politics, reading, watching movies and cooking. She has been teaching at the university level for more than thirty years. Since 1999, she has won seven campus teaching awards and she was inducted into FACET in 2001.

Yi Cheng is a Professor of Mathematical Sciences. She received her Ph.D. in Statistics from The University of Minnesota (1992). She has been teaching at the University level for twenty-four years and has taught more than thirty different courses at the undergraduate and graduate level. She has proposed ten new courses at IU South Bend. She is a recipient of the IU South Bend Distinguished Teaching Award (2012), the Trustees' Teaching Award (2007, 2011), the Teaching Excellence Recognition Award (2000), and the Frederic Bachman Lieber Memorial Award (2012), a highly competitive award across all Indiana University campuses. Yi enjoys teaching, loves her interaction with students, and has served as an adviser for students for more than twelve years. In her free time, she reads, travels, spends time with her family, and works on small home improvement projects.

Alfred J. Guillaume, Jr. was the Executive Vice Chancellor for Academic Affairs and is Professor Emeritus of French. Since retirement he and his wife have traveled extensively in the United States, re-discovering the country's varied physical beauty and its multiple ethnic and regional cultures, and re-acquainting themselves through an extended stay in southern France with its rich cultural and aesthetic history. He is grateful to faculty for allowing him a small part in their creative and teaching lives. As a long-term academic administrator, Alfred has learned that success comes from respect of others and for their views, active listening, empowering others and facilitating their success. He spends his leisure time enjoying ballroom dancing, gardening, traveling, reading, and continuing his research on the francophone literature of people of color in antebellum Louisiana. Academic and administrative honors include a Fulbright Teaching Assistantship in Marseille, France; a W. K. Kellogg National Leadership fellowship; an NEH research grant; and a Carnegie-Mellon for the Humanities grant.

Neovi Karakatsanis is Director of the IU South Bend Honors Program and Professor of Political Science. Inducted into FACET in 2003, Neovi has been the recipient of a Trustees' Teaching Award (2003), the IUSB Distinguished Teaching Award (2008), the IU President's Award for Distinguished Teaching (2008), and the IU South Bend Alumni Association Legacy Award (2009). In 2003, she was also selected as the Student Government Association (SGA) Faculty Member of the Year and received the American Political Science Association's Outstanding Teaching in Political Science award. In addition to teaching courses in international relations and comparative politics, she serves as the president of the Modern Greek Studies Association and writes about Greek society and politics. Currently writing a book on American foreign policy towards Greece at the height of the Cold War, Neovi enjoys traveling internationally and sometimes takes students with her on those trips. She's happy to report that, despite the concerted efforts of some of her most "adventurous" student travelers, Neovi continues to hold her job at IU South Bend and is planning an international trip with honors students.

Tuck Langland is Professor Emeritus of Sculpture at IU South Bend with a total of thirty-nine years teaching at five institutions. Since retirement in 2003 Tuck has remained an active professional sculptor with many large-scale national commissions, and a continuing schedule. As a teacher he prided himself on creating a studio atmosphere where students have no wrong answers, where the only sin is lack of courage in creativity. Thoroughly enjoying retirement, he travels extensively, builds furniture on occasion, writes, sings and swims.

Patricia Lewis, a Motown girl at heart, was born and raised in Detroit and graduated from the University of Michigan with a Bachelor of Science in Mechanical Engineering. Coming from a large family, blessed with a sister with down syndrome, diversity — especially inclusion of special needs — became a passion. During her master's degree at Indiana University, Patricia explored the connections between mathematics and learning disabilities. She thanks her students for teaching her the value of a community classroom where students actively engage with one another. Largely due to this method of teaching, Patricia received the IU South Bend Associate Faculty Distinguished Teaching Award in 2007. She went on to receive the all-campus IU Associate Faculty Distinguished Teaching Award in 2008. She is currently an Associate Faculty of Mathematical Sciences. In her free time, she enjoys watching sports, especially her children at cross-country or soccer. She feels that we should celebrate our blessings each day. Though she started her career as an aerospace engineer, after twenty-two years as an adjunct professor of math, she now finds teaching "out of this world!"

Gwynn Mettetal is Chancellor's Professor of Psychology and Education, teaching courses in child development, educational psychology, and research methods. She is Director of the University Center for Excellence in Teaching and is particularly interested in mentoring and career development. In her free time, she reads, entertains, and provides tech support to the rest of her family. Gwynn would like to thank all of the students who have taught her so much through their (usually tactful) feedback. She has been teaching at the university level for 40 years, and hopes to "get it right" before she retires. Teaching awards include FACET, IUSB Distinguished Teaching Award, IU Distinguished Teaching Award, and four Trustees' Teaching Awards.

Sara Sage was Associate Professor of Secondary Education and is now in full-time private practice as a Licensed Mental Health Counselor. Sara received the FACET award and several Trustees' Teaching Awards during her tenure at IU South Bend. Sara, an INFJ in the Myers-Briggs Type Indicator personality inventory, would like to thank her son, an INTP, and any ESTJ/ESTP students — K-12 or college — over the years for teaching her that not everyone likes to process things endlessly the way she does. To prepare authentic teachers in these times of a more standardized and mechanized focus in K-12 education requires a strong commitment to a humanistic approach, and Sara thanks her mentors Vince Peterson and Randy Isaacson for helping her shape her approach to the F-201 course over the last nineteen years. Vince — in spirit — and Randy — in your own private Idaho — this one's for you!

P. N. Saksena received his Ph.D. in Accounting from Georgia State University and his master's degree in accounting from University of Georgia. He is a Fellow Chartered Accountant. He completed his Bachelor's in Commerce (Honors) from Delhi University in India.

At IU South Bend, he was Professor of Accounting. He was Associate Dean for Graduate Programs and Accreditation before he became Interim Dean of the Judd Leighton School of Business and Economics. His teaching interests include management accounting, auditing and forensic accounting. His scholarship interests are in the fields of forensic accounting and accounting education. He enjoys student-related service the most. In July 2017, he became Dean of the College of Business Administration at Winthrop University. He has taught at the university level for twenty-five years and has enjoyed connecting with students. He has been honored with more than 20 teaching awards including IU South Bend Alumni Association Faculty Legacy Award, IU President's Award for Excellence in Teaching, IU South Bend Distinguished Teaching Award, Faculty of the Year Award, and [co-recipient] Outstanding Educator of the Year Award. He has also been inducted into FACET.

Carolyn A. Schult is an Associate Professor of Psychology, specializing in developmental psychology. She teaches courses in both child and lifespan developmental psychology, introductory psychology, a senior capstone research course, and to keep things interesting, a general education course featuring an intensive historical role-playing game set in colonial New York. Carolyn enjoys cooking, reading, and spending time with her family, who enjoy spending time with Carolyn, reading, and ordering take-out. She received the IU South Bend Alumni Association Legacy Award, Trustees' Teaching Award (four-time winner) and is a member of FACET.

Monica Maria Tetzlaff is an Associate Professor of History and teaches in the African-American Studies, Women's Studies, and Sustainability programs. She is a fan of place-based education, and has led students on African-American history tours of South Bend and also takes her students on nature and history-based walks around the campus and in community parks. Monica is a former Director of the Civil Rights Heritage Center and she continues to research and write about human rights history in the U.S. and in Ghana. She has received Trustees' Teaching Awards and community service awards such as the Eldon Lundquist award. She is also a FACET member. Recently she received a Fulbright Fellowship to teach in the African Institute at the University of Ghana. Monica is constantly learning from her students, especially when they travel together "out in the field" outside the classroom.

Tom Vander Ven is Professor Emeritus of English and taught American Literature and creative writing at Indiana University South Bend for his entire career from 1967 to 2001. He received the all-Indiana University Herman Frederic Lieber Memorial Award for excellence in teaching in 1985 and the IU South Bend Eldon F. Lundquist Award in 1991. His university service included terms as chair of the Department of English, of the Academic Senate, and of the Athletics Committee. Twelve of his plays were produced in Indiana, Michigan, and Virginia. His publications include poetry, essays, and two books. His most recent essay, "The Secret Lives of the Elderly," appeared in *Currents*, the journal of the College of Liberal Arts and Sciences at IU South Bend.

Jay VanderVeen is Associate Professor and Chair of the Department of Sociology and Anthropology. He has won recognition for his teaching eight times, including the IU South Bend Distinguished Teaching Award and the Indiana University Herman Frederic Lieber Memorial Award. Additionally, he received a commendation for being an outstanding faculty mentor. He stays constantly busy teaching courses from ancient civilization to zombies. As an archaeologist, he likes to get out of the classroom and work with students in the field. He regularly supervises excavations and internships, and can never pass up a museum visit. He relishes the opportunity to study a host of topics (which makes him an ideal team trivia member) and the experience of learning from his many students.

About the Editors

Marianne Castano Bishop completed her doctorate and master's degree in human development and psychology at the Harvard University Graduate School of Education. She also holds a master's degree in educational foundations from Boston College and another master's degree in counseling and human services, specializing in clinical mental health counseling from Indiana University South Bend. She is currently a Licensed Mental Health Counselor Associate.

At IU South Bend she started as the Instructional Strategist at the University Center for Excellence in Teaching. She later became the Distance Learning Program Manager and was promoted to founding Director of the Center for Distance Education, now the Center for Online Education. She is also the Director of Off-Campus Programs. As adjunct faculty at IU South Bend, she taught several courses offered through the departments of Psychology and Computer Science as well as the School of Education.

Her consultations with faculty inspired her to start the publication of this book and to submit a proposal for funding with the Academic Senate's Budget Committee at that time. It was approved by the committee and then-Chancellor Una Mae Reck.

She enjoys spending time with her family, their long-haired cat Silky, and papillon dog Bodhi. She is learning to play the guitar and piano (again), and percussion cajon, reading, writing poetry, painting, and designing and creating jewelry mobiles.

Gwendolyn (Gwynn) Mettetal has a Ph.D. in Developmental Psychology from the University of Illinois at Urbana-Champaign. She earned her master's in psychology and bachelor's degrees in psychology and sociology at East Tennessee State University.

At IU South Bend, she is Chancellor's Professor of Psychology and Education.

P. N. Saksena received his Ph.D. in Accounting from Georgia State University and his Master's in Accounting from University of Georgia. He is a Fellow Chartered Accountant. He completed his Bachelor in Commerce degree with honors from Delhi University in India.

At IU South Bend, he was Professor of Accounting at the Judd Leighton School of Business and Economics. He was Associate Dean of Graduate Programs and Accreditation before he became Interim Dean.

91924274R00104

Made in the USA
Columbia, SC
27 March 2018